SOUTHERN
— FROM —
SCRATCH

SOUTHERN
— FROM —
SCRATCH
PANTRY ESSENTIALS AND DOWN-HOME RECIPES

ASHLEY ENGLISH

PHOTOGRAPHS BY JOHNNY AUTRY

ROOST BOOKS
BOULDER
2018

Roost Books
An imprint of Shambhala Publications, Inc.
4720 Walnut Street
Boulder, Colorado 80301
roostbooks.com

9 8 7 6 5 4 3 2 1

First Edition
Printed in China

∞ This edition is printed on acid-free paper that meets the American National Standards Institute Z39.48 Standard.
♻ Shambhala Publications makes every effort to print on recycled paper.
For more information please visit www.shambhala.com.

Distributed in the United States by Penguin Random House LLC and in Canada by Random House of Canada Ltd

Designed by Allison Meierding

Library of Congress Cataloging-in-Publication Data

Names: English, Ashley, 1976– author. | Autry, Johnny, photographer.
Title: Southern from scratch: pantry essentials and down-home recipes / Ashley English; photographs by Johnny Autry.
Description: First edition. | Boulder, Colorado: Roost Books, an imprint of Shambhala Publications, Inc., [2018] | Includes index.
Identifiers: LCCN 2017013852 | ISBN 9781611803310 (hardcover: alk. paper)
Subjects: LCSH: Cooking, American—Southern style. | Cooking—Southern States. | Appalachian Region, Southern.
Classification: LCC TX715.2.S68 E48 2018 | DDC 641.5975—dc23
LC record available at https://lccn.loc.gov/2017013852

To Nanny and Mamaw, for showing me the beauty
in a can of bacon drippings, a pan of hot biscuits,
and a jar of bread & butter pickles.

CONTENTS

INTRODUCTION

————

I wasn't always smitten by Southern foods. If you had told me when I was twenty years old that, two decades later, I'd be writing a hefty book on creating a Southern foods pantry, I'd have denied even the mere possibility. Though I grew up in a Southern kitchen with a strong legacy of female cooks crafting memorable meals, and though I was deeply interested in food, cooking, and spending time in the kitchen in general, directing my attention to the culinary heritage of my upbringing was about as far off my radar as imaginable.

My mother, Diane, grandmother Ruby Marie (my "Nanny"), and great-grandmother Lena May ("Mamaw") all hail from Henry County, Virginia. The Southern Appalachian mountain towns of Bassett and Martinsville were their specific stomping grounds. I have vivid associations with locations in the form of foods, and perhaps more specifically, food aromas. When we would visit Mamaw, her home always smelled like bacon and biscuits. Even now, those scents instantly transport me to her linoleum-tiled kitchen, to her porch swing, and to the intense quietness of the house she shared for most of her life with her husband, my Papaw.

My family eventually made its way east, to the up-and-coming cities of Chesapeake and Virginia Beach, Virginia. It was at Nanny's U-pick blueberry farm in Chesapeake that I first learned about keeping a flock of backyard chickens, putting up jars of pickles and jams, and growing a kitchen garden. My mother, a single mom influenced by the convenience foods of the eighties, understandably toggled between her Southern foods upbringing and the expediency of Tuna Helper and Manwich.

My time with these three women created deep, formative, indelible memories, ultimately placing me at the intersection of history and modernity, of looking to the past and utilizing the tools available in the present. As I entered my late teens and prepared for college, I became increasingly concerned about recurrent health issues in my family. Diabetes, heart disease, and obesity continued to evidence themselves, and, in an effort to avoid inheriting those particular family traits, I began what would become a lifetime interest in nutrition.

Over the next fifteen years, I pursued vegan, vegetarian, macrobiotic, and raw food diets. I worked in small mom-and-pop natural foods stores and for nationwide natural foods chains. In my passion for natural health and living, I even obtained a bachelor's degree in holistic nutrition. Throughout it all, however, I felt physically horrible, my stomach seemingly always under siege, my reproductive health endlessly challenged, my energy levels plagued by lethargy and fatigue.

It wasn't until I'd met and married my husband, Glenn, that things began to change. During the spring of 2010, while pregnant with our son Huxley, I turned to him one day, and, out of nowhere, declared that I wanted a cheeseburger. Mind you, at that point, I'd been vegetarian for fourteen years, having only recently introduced a bit of poultry and seafood to my diet. It was profound, this craving for meat.

It was also during this time that I began to desire whole fats again. For years, I adopted the low-fat diet advocated by doctors far and wide. I used vegan margarine, drank low-fat soy milk, and largely abstained from cheese. I was working at that time as a nutrition consultant and medical assistant for a doctor in Asheville, North Carolina. His dietary approach was entirely different from the one I was engaging in. Essentially, his was all about whole foods—whole fats, whole grains, and whole animal products. I attended a conference on the subject, and slowly began incorporating this approach into my own diet. It felt amazing. This was the best I had felt in years, decades even.

As I brought these foods back into my life, I realized that I'd pretty much wholesale discarded my entire culinary background. It had been years since I'd eaten grits, bacon, biscuits, pimento cheese, or deviled eggs (for shame!) out of fear that my health would follow the path of my family's. Reintroducing whole foods into my diet, though, and having profound positive changes in my health, made me realize that it wasn't Southern foods that had caused my family so much trouble. Instead, it was the processed foods that had weaseled their way in, and undermined my family's culinary legacy in turn.

And so, the circle was made whole again. I had walked away from Mamaw's bacon and Nanny's bread-and-butter pickles thinking I was doing the right thing, not realizing that I was discarding an entire history of nutritious, sustaining, delicious foods in the process, not to mention the stories and family histories that went with them. Nanny passed away while I was working on this book, on December 20, 2015. She was ninety years old, and just as vibrant and willful and silly as she'd always been. It was an absolute pleasure to discuss her influence on my culinary career, and her own Southern foods upbringing, before she passed. I am ever grateful for the role she played in my life, as well as for my mom for keeping the flame alive, even when I was the one wanting to extinguish it.

The book I offer you here is a culmination of my life's work, really. It synthesizes the foods I grew up with, information I learned during my time pursuing my nutrition degree, and what I've gathered working for the past decade in my home kitchen with my husband, Glenn, an innovative and masterful home cook. Those three arenas—childhood, study, married life—are distilled in this book into my current approach to Southern cooking. Whole, natural foods, looking to the region and the history of cooking in the Southern Appalachians, with its emphasis on seasonal produce and slow cooking—that's how I cook. The apple, as they say, never falls far from the tree. In my case, the apple might've rolled down the hill a bit and planted herself beside a wild apple tree, but she never really left the orchard.

CREATING A SOUTHERN FOODS PANTRY

Creating a Southern foods pantry might come naturally to you. Perhaps, like me, you're a true GRITS ("Girl Raised in the South"). You've been watching your grandmother put up jar upon jar of bread-and-butter pickles and your mom whip up a batch of buttermilk biscuits for as long as you can remember. Or perhaps you've come to the cuisine of the South by vocation, relationship, or mere curiosity. Whatever brought you to this book, whether family tree or love of bacon, my goal is to showcase what I consider the fundamental elements of creating a from-scratch, all-natural, fully delicious Southern foods pantry.

How to Use This Book

When I first began writing this book, I kept returning to the idea that basic, abiding, consistent elements are found in most every kitchen of the Southern Appalachians, my stomping grounds. You will always find buttermilk, grits, lard, and chow chow. Hot pepper jelly, breakfast sausage, and pickled okra appear on restaurant menus and kitchen tables alike. Sure, various iterations and permutations and interpretations appear along the way, but these staples are constant.

Using those basics as my starting point, I created eight categories—a veritable grocery store's worth of designations. Pickles & Relishes, Jams & Spreads, Sauces & Vinegars, Fruits & Vegetables, Dry Goods & Sundries, Fats & Meats, Icebox & Freezer, and Sweeteners & Desserts offer fifty base recipes for crafting your Southern foods pantry. From Applesauce (page 102) to Picked Watermelon Rind (page 47), it's all there. The base recipes are listed at the beginning of each chapter, as well as noted throughout the chapter.

From there, I offer additional suggestions for use. Having authored a book on preserving foods myself, as well as owning and reading countless other books on the topic, I knew that, well, sometimes once you've got that jar of jam, it's lovely to know what to do with it aside from spreading it liberally across buttered toast. To that end, I created two, sometimes three, iterations for incorporating those biscuits, potato chips, dilly beans, or lard into composed dishes. Furthermore, these base recipes appear within other recipes throughout the book, thereby reinforcing just how essential they are to my Southern pantry.

While hewing closely to the flavor profile of Southern cuisine, I stayed true to the way that I cook in my own Southern kitchen. You'll find Buttermilk & Smoky Paprika Fried Chicken (page 200) alongside dishes that are vegetarian, gluten-free, and multicultural in ingredient. I'll show you how to take those tomatoes you canned on page 120 and turn them into a Southern Shakshuka on page 123, bringing a bit of North African flavor to your Southern table. Or how to delight your friends and family with Poached Pears with Pound Cake, Candied Black Walnuts, and Bourbon Whipped Cream (page 230). Essentially, my aim is to get you comfortable with creating the nuts and bolts, the *foundation*, of a Southern pantry, and then inspire you with fresh, modern ways to incorporate them into your kitchen.

Ingredients and Equipment

While you will likely recognize most of the ingredients in this book, I call regularly for several items that merit a bit of detail if you are unaccustomed to them. Likewise for the equipment. While most of you own mixing bowls and rimmed baking pans, you may be less acquainted with a few of the kitchen items that I use. Any ingredients that you can't find locally are easily sourced online or via mail order (see Resources (page 239) for some suggestions). Let the introductions begin!

INGREDIENTS

COUNTRY HAM

For the uninitiated the first bite of country ham can come as a bit of a shock. A type of cured meat, country ham is preserved through salting, typically for 1 to 3 months, followed by smoking and aging. The end result is a very salty ham. Unlike "city ham," which has a sweet flavor and is typically eaten in thick, large slices, country ham comes in thin slices and is served in small amounts.

CORNMEAL

Made from dried corn, cornmeal is available in several formats. Fine, medium, and coarse grinding results in a meal of variable texture, and, resultantly, mouthfeel when eaten. When I call for cornmeal in this book, I always indicate which format to use. Whether to use yellow or white cornmeal is entirely up to you.

GRITS

Technically known as "hominy grits," grits are also made from dried corn. Their texture, however, is considerably coarser than cornmeal. Like cornmeal, grits are available in both white and yellow varieties. Whatever you choose, just be sure to avoid "quick grits," as those have had the germ and hull of the corn kernels removed, resulting in a considerably reduced corn flavor.

PICKLING SALT

Pickling salt is simply sodium chloride that lacks anti-caking ingredients. Such additives can cloud the brine, while others, such as iodine, can darken pickles. When salt is called for in canned goods, use one labeled "pickling," "canning," or "kosher."

SMOKED SEA SALT

I call for smoked sea salt in a number of recipes. It is a wonderful way of imparting a smoky flavor, which I simply adore, to foods. That said, if you don't care for or can't find smoked sea salt, regular sea salt works equally well.

SORGHUM SYRUP

Once the most common sweetener in the Southern Appalachians alongside honey, sorghum syrup is made from the boiled stalks of sorghum grass. This crop has a naturally high sugar content and grows well in the mountainous terrain and rolling hills of the Southern Appalachian region. Sometimes referred to as "sorghum molasses," the phrase is misleading, as true molasses is a by-product of sugarcane and sugar beet production.

SUMAC

A flowering plant in the genus *Rhus*, sumac can be found throughout the world. The plant grows wild all over the Southern Appalachians, where it has a long history of culinary use. Ground into a fine powder, the fruits, known as "drupes," are used as a spice, imparting a tart, lemon-like flavor to dishes. Southerners also frequently use the whole fruits to create a lemonade-like beverage called "sumac-ade."

EQUIPMENT

CAST IRON SKILLET

My great-grandmother Lena May, grandmother Ruby Marie, and mother Diane all worshipped at the altar of the cast iron skillet. No stainless-steel pots and pans for them, thank you. Suffice to say, when it came time to begin amassing my own kitchen equipment, cast iron was the only way I thought to go. Today, my kitchen equally employs both cast iron and stainless-steel vessels. In this book, I frequently call for using cast iron because of its durability, iconic association with Southern food (call me sentimental!), and heat-retention abilities. Cast iron is a powerhouse when it comes to staying hot once heated. The downside, however, is that it can take a bit of time to heat up evenly, which is especially important when heating meats. So, when I call for a cast iron skillet, let it warm up for a good 10 minutes before you begin cooking in it. Of course, if you don't own a cast iron skillet, you can always use stainless steel (or ask Santa to bring you one come the holidays). It's important to clean and maintain your cast iron cookware properly, otherwise it will rust and foods will stick to it. If you aren't familiar with cast iron care, I encourage you to look over the manual that comes with your item, or read up on the subject online.

MASON JARS

A type of molded glass jar used in home canning, the Mason jar was named after its inventor, John Landis Mason. Created in 1858, Mason jars are fashioned from tempered glass and are able to withstand repeated use in high-temperature environments, such as those found in water bath and pressure canning. Mason jars have a threaded mouth and are intended to be used with accompanying lids and screw bands, which hold the jar's contents inside during processing. While the jars are reusable, permitted they have no cracks or scratches, the lids are meant for single use, though you can reuse the screw bands repeatedly so long as they haven't rusted. (European-style canning jars using two-piece glass jars and lids, held in place with wire hinges or clamps, are now also widely available for purchase.) Available in wide or regular "mouth," Mason jars are offered in a range of volumes, including quarter-pint, half-pint, pint, quart, and half-gallon.

SLOW COOKER

A number of the recipes in this book feature the use of a slow cooker. If you don't own a slow cooker, I highly recommend that you purchase one. The peace of mind that comes from letting a piece of meat slowly cook away while you go about your business is hard to beat. A range of models and prices can be found in stores and online. Find one that best suits your preferences and budget and then care for it like the precious jewel it is. One seasoned tip: never pour cold liquids into a hot cooker. I once mistakenly did this, only to hear the heartbreaking snap and ping of the porcelain insert cracking. Warm foods into a warm cooker, or warm/hot foods into a room temperature cooker that is then turned on are totally fine, while cold foods into a hot cooker are not. Live and learn, eh?

Preservation Techniques

Creating a Southern pantry necessarily involves preserving foods. Though not difficult to learn to do or perform, some aspects of food preservation require a thorough understanding to be done safely and correctly. Here are detailed steps on how to water bath can, freeze fruits and vegetables, and store potatoes and onions.

HOW TO WATER BATH CAN

The boiling water bath processing method is used for high-acid foods, including jams, jellies, marmalades, preserves, pickles, relishes, chutneys, salsas, ketchup, some sauces, and tomatoes. These items require a temperature of 212°F in order to kill off harmful microorganisms, and the boiling water bath provides just such an environment.

Assemble your equipment. Gather jars, closures, canner and rack, jar lifter, funnel, spatula, recipe ingredients—everything you'll need to concoct your recipe, bottle it up, and process it. While you're at it, read through your recipe. Know what you're getting into, how many jars it yields, and how much time you should be prepared to spend on the entire process.

Examine all jars, lids, and screw bands. Whether you are using new jars or those that have seen the inside of a canning pot many times, inspect the rims for cracks, nicks, or uneven edges (I run my index finger around the circumference of the jar). Although it is unlikely that new jars will have faults, it is not entirely impossible, and weeding out the duds at this point saves you from leaks and messes later. Check your screw bands, too. If you're reusing any, discard those that have rusted or show signs of wear, such as scratches or scuff marks.

Heat the jars. Fill your canner with enough water to cover the filled jars by 1 to 2 inches. If the rack you are using has handles, fill it with jars and then use the handles to lower the rack into the canner. Otherwise (such as when using a cake cooling rack), put it directly into the canner and then add the jars you will be using. Allow the jars to fill with water. Cover and heat until almost boiling, around 180°F. Keep the jars hot and the canner covered until ready to begin filling.

Prepare your recipe. If you are following a recipe with an especially lengthy cooking and preparation time, it is wise to wait until you are finished, or at least on the home stretch, before you start warming up your jars and lids. Otherwise, you'll be using unnecessary energy keeping everything at just under boiling the entire time. I've tried my best to indicate when to begin the boiling water bath in each recipe.

Fill the jars.
1. Using a jar lifter, carefully remove one jar at a time from the canner, taking care to tip out the water away from you and back into the pot.

2. Place the empty jar on a kitchen towel or wood cutting board on the counter; avoid direct contact between a hot jar and a cold surface, such as a marble or granite countertop, which could cause the jar to crack.

3. Pour the recipe contents into a container with a pouring spout, such as a pitcher or large glass-measuring cup, before filling the individual jars. You could skip this step if you prefer, but as a petite, small-framed woman I find it helpful to avoid pouring directly from a large pot.

4. Place a canning funnel over a jar and fill until there is either ¼ inch or ½ inch headspace—the space between the top of the food in the jar and the underside of the lid—depending on what your recipe indicates. Generally, whole fruits and any pickled and acidified foods (such as chutneys, relishes, pickles, condiments, and tomatoes) require ½ inch headspace, whereas fruit spreads and juices need ¼ inch headspace. Changes in altitude don't affect headspace amounts.

5. Using a nonmetallic spatula or chopstick, release any trapped air bubbles inside the jar. Check the headspace again and adjust as needed. Too much headspace can prevent a proper vacuum seal from forming, while too little can cause the contents of the jar to boil out during processing.

Clean the jar rims. Wipe the rim and threads of each jar with a clean, dampened kitchen cloth, removing any food debris that may have dripped when filling.

Place lids and screw bands on jars. Center lids atop each jar and secure with a screw band. Turn each screw band until you feel a little bit of resistance, and then continue twisting on until it is fingertip-tight, meaning the point at which your fingertips alone can undo the screw band. Be sure you don't overtighten the screw bands; doing so can prevent the jars from venting properly during processing, which can in turn jeopardize the formation of a thorough seal.

Process the jars. Using a jar lifter, place the filled jars one at a time into the canner. Be certain they are sitting on top of the rack and aren't touching each other, since you want the boiling water to circulate underneath, over, and in between each jar. Once all jars are in the canner, adjust the water level as needed to ensure all jars are covered by 1 to 2 inches. Place the lid on the canner and bring the water to a full, rolling boil. Once the water reaches a sustained boil, you can begin timing. The water must continue boiling rapidly for the entire duration of the processing.

Adjust for altitude. Altitude affects the temperature at which water boils. Basically, air becomes less dense the higher up you go from sea level, and air with reduced density exerts less pressure. While sea level water boils at 212°F, it boils at a lower temperature at a higher altitude. In home canning, molds and yeasts are killed and enzymes that cause spoilage are deactivated at 212°F. In order to circumvent that issue at a higher altitude, some additional processing time is needed. If you're at sea level, follow the time called for in the recipe. From 1,000–3,000 feet above sea level, add 5 minutes; 3,001–6,000 feet, add 10 minutes; 6,001–8,000 feet, add 15 minutes; and 8,001–10,000 feet, add 20 minutes.

Cool the jars. After the processing time is complete, turn off the heat and take the lid off the canner. Remove the jars one at a time with a jar lifter. Place them on a kitchen cloth on the counter and allow them to cool, untouched, for several hours.

Check the seals. If you heard lots of popping and pinging coming from your jars as they cooled, you're pretty much guaranteed success, although you'll still need to visibly and physically determine whether each jar is sealed. Remove the screw bands from the jars, dry them thoroughly, and return them to the pantry. (Screw bands serve no function after processing, and should be removed to help prevent rusting caused by water drops wedged between the screw band and the jar threads.) Next, view your jars from the side, looking for a slight indentation in the center of the lid. Press down on the lid with your fingertips and feel around for a downward-curving dent. A properly sealed lid will remain in place once you remove your finger, refusing to yield. Grasp your jar by the lid only, checking to see if it remains firmly attached. If your lid springs back when pushed on, slips off either partially or completely, or shows no indentation, you will need to reprocess or refrigerate.

Label and store. Label and date your jars while their contents are fresh in your mind. For the best flavor and texture, eat your homemade wares within 1 year. While those items over 1 year might not have necessarily gone bad, the quality will begin to suffer. Many home canners use a permanent magic marker, writing directly on the lid for easy identification. You can also use labels and stickers if you'd like your goods to stay pretty for quick gift giving. Store in a cool, dry, darkened location, such as a pantry, cabinet, or basement. Home-canned goods need to be kept between 40°F and 70°F in an area free from high humidity.

HOW TO FREEZE FRUITS AND VEGETABLES

If you have access to a farmers' market, or maintain your own kitchen garden, a highly economical way to extend your pantry is by freezing fruits and vegetables. Stored in airtight freezer bags or lidded freezer containers, frozen fruits and vegetables will last about 1 year (while they're still safe after a year, their overall taste and texture will begin to deteriorate).

FREEZING FRUITS

Quickly rinse your fruits and compost any damaged, bruised, or otherwise compromised specimens. Pit stone fruits like cherries, peaches, nectarines, and apricots and then cut the larger fruits into even slices and transfer them to freezer bags or freezer containers. Arrange berries in a single layer on a rimmed baking sheet, place in the freezer until frozen, and then transfer to freezer bags or containers. Remember to label and date each container.

FREEZING VEGETABLES

Vegetables do best with a quick blanch before freezing to keep enzymes and microorganisms from damaging the vegetable's color, flavor, and nutrients. Chop the vegetables, drop them in rapidly boiling water for about 30 seconds, and then quickly submerge them in an ice water bath. Remove from the water and dry thoroughly on paper towels or kitchen cloths. Once dry, store the vegetables snugly in labeled and dated freezer bags or freezer containers. The more tightly packed they are, the less air contact the vegetables will have, which helps prevent dreaded freezer burn.

HOW TO STORE POTATOES AND ONIONS

The potato and onion bin of my childhood stands out with profound clarity. I even remember the day my mom bought it at a craft fair in Chesapeake, Virginia. On top was a sturdy wooden potato bin cradled by a slanted lid, while the onion drawer rested below. "Taters" and "Onions" were written in loopy white letters on their respective stations, the cursive hinting at treasured gemstones inside, not earth-covered tubers and fragrant alliums. That bin got loads of mileage, literally, moving with us from Virginia across the length of North Carolina, twice. To this day, it sits sturdily in my mom's kitchen, holding its precious cargo at the ready.

Potatoes and onions can be put away for short- or long-term storage, depending on your needs and specific storage conditions. Short term, you can keep them at room temperature, away from light. A bin akin to my mom's would work just fine, permitted the potatoes and onions don't get too hot, are kept in the dark at all times, and aren't stored for too long (2 weeks maximum).

Otherwise, for long-term storage, you'll need a root cellar, basement, or unused closet that can be climate-controlled. Seek out varieties known to store well. Once cured, store in bushel baskets or ventilated bins covered with newspaper or cardboard to block out all light. You can store potatoes and onions near each other but not together, as they each contain chemicals that can cause the other to rot. Ideal potato storage temperature is between 35°F and 40°F (although they'll still store for a few months up to 50°F) and for onions between 35°F and 45°F. So, store them in the same area around 40°F to 45°F and you're in good shape. Remove any moldy or limp produce immediately.

1

PICKLES
— & —
RELISHES

CHOW CHOW

A type of pickled relish, chow chow has been a part of the Southern Appalachian culinary canon since the early 1800s. Its multipurpose "soup pot" nature makes it a popular means of using up any available vegetable, though cabbage does appear rather consistently. Along with ingredients, chow chow also varies in relative levels of sweetness, some being considerably sweeter than others. My "Goldilocks" version is neither too sweet nor too sour.

The etymology of the term "chow chow" is widely disputed. Some believe it hails from the Chinese word *cha*, meaning mixed; others argue it stems from the Indian word for chayote squash, a common ingredient in a popular Indian pickle; another viewpoint claims an association with the French word for cabbage, *chou*. Those maintaining the Chinese origin of the word believe Chinese immigrant laborers brought it to California. The European lineage claim links chow chow to the Acadians of Nova Scotia, who brought it with them during their migration to Louisiana. Regardless of where the name stems from and how it ended up in the South, chow chow stayed put once it appeared on the Southern culinary scene and can now be found in kitchens, pantries, and restaurants across the region.

As a Southerner, I have known of chow chow my entire life. It wasn't a condiment my family canned on the regular, but I have always been aware of its presence. My husband, Glenn, and I love it, and find all manner of uses for tucking it in here and there. Like most pickles and relishes, chow chow does best with some aging time once jarred. Hold out for at least 2 weeks before sampling; 1 month is ideal.

SERVING SUGGESTIONS

- *The vinegary bite of chow chow would be an excellent foil to the sweetness of Watermelon Rind Sloppy Joes (page 49); heap a generous forkful onto each serving.*
- *Use as a topping for Southern-Style Pinto Beans (page 167), served alongside butter-slathered hunks of Cornbread (page 142).*
- *Dollop generously atop Hoppin' John (page 169).*

CHOW CHOW

· MAKES ABOUT 3 PINTS ·

---

1 small head green cabbage, grated	1 cup apple cider vinegar (see Note)
1 medium cucumber, peeled and finely chopped	⅔ cup light brown sugar
1 medium onion, diced	½ cup water
1 red bell pepper, diced	2 teaspoons mustard powder
¼ cup pickling salt	1 teaspoon ground turmeric
	1 teaspoon celery seeds

NOTE: **As per the note about the variable acidity of homemade apple cider vinegar on page 90, use store-bought vinegar here (since the jars will be water bath canned), or purchase pH strips and perform an acidity test.**

1. Combine the cabbage, cucumber, onion, bell pepper, and pickling salt in a large nonreactive mixing bowl, such as glass or ceramic. Using clean hands, toss the vegetables with the salt to fully combine. Cover loosely with a kitchen cloth and leave at room temperature for 8 to 12 hours.
2. Drain the mixture in a colander, pressing on the vegetables with a wooden or metal spoon. Don't rinse with water, though, just press out and discard any juices.
3. Combine the vinegar, brown sugar, water, mustard powder, turmeric, and celery seeds in a medium pot. Stir over medium heat until the sugar has fully dissolved. Add the vegetable mixture, stir to combine, and bring to a boil. Reduce the heat and simmer for 15 minutes.
4. While the chow chow cooks, fill a canner or large stockpot with water, place three or four pint jars inside, and set over medium-high heat. Bring just to the boiling point.
5. Using a jar lifter, remove the hot jars from the canner and place on top of a kitchen cloth on the counter. With the help of a canning funnel, pack the chow chow into the jars, reserving ½ inch headspace.
6. Use a spatula or wooden chopstick to remove any trapped air bubbles around the interior circumference of the jars. Wipe the rims clean with a damp cloth. Place the lids and screw bands on the jars, tightening only until fingertip-tight.
7. Again using a jar lifter, slowly place the filled jars in the canner. Be sure that the jars are covered by at least 1 inch of water. Bring to a boil, and then process for 10 minutes, starting the timer once the water is at a full, rolling boil. Adjust for altitude as needed (see page 9 for detailed canning instructions).

SOUTHERN GREENS WITH CHOW CHOW
· SERVES 6 TO 8 ·

Greens served alongside a bit of chow chow are a Southern classic. Add some Southern-Style Pinto Beans (page 167) and a skillet of Cornbread (page 142) and you've got the makings of a Southern Appalachian dinner. I use a ham hock in my greens, as I find the flavor the meat imparts does wonders to the potlikker, the soupy broth surrounding the greens. Source ham hocks from a trusted butcher in your area; if you don't see them on the menu, ask about having some smoked to order.

2 large bunches turnip or collard greens, stems removed, leaves torn into large pieces
1 teaspoon sea salt, plus more to taste
1½-pound ham hock

1 tablespoon Lard (page 173) or Bacon Drippings (page 176)
Chow Chow, to serve

1. Fill the sink with cold water. Submerge the greens and agitate them in the water. Drain the sink with the greens still in it, refill with water, and repeat.
2. Bring 2 quarts of cold water to a boil in a large pot or Dutch oven. Add the salt. Begin adding the greens, in fistfuls, waiting for them to wilt with each batch. Add the ham hock and lard, and stir to combine.
3. Reduce the heat to medium-low. Position a lid on top of the pot so that the pot isn't fully covered. Simmer for 2 hours, or until the greens have wilted and the ham is falling off the bone.
4. Remove the ham hock. Pick out the meat, cutting up any large pieces, and return it to the pot. Discard the bone.
5. Add salt to taste, and serve hot, with Chow Chow.

PICKLED SHRIMP & CHOW CHOW
· SERVES 4 TO 6 ·

Making pickled shrimp couldn't be easier. Peeling and deveining the shrimp is a time-consuming task, but one that I truly love (a perfect activity to do while listening to a beloved podcast!). Everything goes into a bowl, gets stirred, and then refrigerated. Four hours later, you pull it out and your delicious appetizer is good to go. If you're feeding a crowd, I'd aim for 4 pounds of shrimp and scale up the other ingredients accordingly.

1 pound shell-on medium shrimp

1 medium sweet onion, thinly sliced

½ lemon, thinly sliced

¼ cup Apple Cider Vinegar (page 88)

¼ cup extra-virgin olive oil

2 tablespoons capers

2 teaspoons sea salt

1 teaspoon celery seeds

Several dashes of hot sauce

¼ teaspoon smoked paprika

¼ cup celery leaves

Freshly ground black pepper

Chow Chow, to serve

1. Bring a large pot of salted water to a boil. Add the shrimp and boil just until opaque, about 2 minutes.
2. Transfer the shrimp to a colander and drain, rinsing with cold water. Peel and devein the shrimp, leaving the tails intact.
3. In a medium glass or ceramic mixing bowl, combine the shrimp with the onion, lemon, vinegar, olive oil, capers, salt, celery seeds, hot sauce, paprika, celery leaves, and black pepper to taste. Stir to fully combine.
4. Cover the bowl with a plate or lid and chill for at least 4 hours in the refrigerator. Take out of the refrigerator 10 to 15 minutes before serving.
5. To serve, spoon a bit of the pickled shrimp mixture onto a small plate and top with chow chow. The shrimp flesh and chow chow are eaten together, and the tails are discarded.

BREAD & BUTTER PICKLES

Bread-and-butter pickles were one of my grandmother Nanny's pantry staples, and are now one of mine. I am as grateful to Nanny for teaching me how to make these as I am my mother for teaching me how to drive a car (in a manual SUV, in the mountains of western North Carolina; no small feat, mind you). They're just that good.

The origin of the pickle's name is somewhat disputed. I've read that it comes from the pickles being sandwiched between slices of buttered bread, offered as a meal during times of financial duress or scarcity. There's also mention of an Illinois farming couple who bartered their homemade sweet and sour pickles (named "Fanning's Bread and Butter Pickles") with their local grocer for bread and butter during economic downturns.

I can clearly recall waiting in Nanny's Chesapeake, Virginia, kitchen while jars of her bread-and-butter pickles boiled in the pot. She'd make me a bowl of white rice and butter, sprinkled with white sugar (notable in its simplicity and for being strangely delicious), and we'd pass the time waiting for the timer to ding eating our rice and chatting about whatever trivialities young girls fret and fuss over.

To this day, whenever I put up some pints of bread-and-butter pickles, or open up a fresh jar, I associate the sweet pickle with my grandmother. She learned how to make them from her mother, who likely learned from her own mother. With these pickles, I'm not just preserving my harvest of cucumbers and peppers, I'm preserving my family's history as well.

SERVING SUGGESTIONS

- *Pulled pork needs a little acid to balance it out. Make Pulled Pork sliders (page 95) and layer the pickles on top.*
- *Chop into bite-sized pieces and incorporate into a chicken salad with a bit of mayonnaise and some Dijon mustard.*
- *Serve as an element of a pickle platter—alongside Pickled Okra (page 27), Pickled Beets (page 24), and some sharp cheddar and aged Gouda—or an Appalachian Ploughman's Lunch (page 133).*

BREAD & BUTTER PICKLES

· MAKES ABOUT 4 PINTS ·

4 pounds pickling cucumbers

1 large red bell pepper, chopped

1 large sweet onion, chopped

¼ cup pickling salt

3 cups apple cider vinegar (see Note)

1 cup packed light brown sugar

2 tablespoons yellow mustard seeds

2 teaspoons red pepper flakes

1 teaspoon celery seeds

1 teaspoon ground turmeric

½ teaspoon ground cloves

NOTE: As per the note about the variable acidity of homemade apple cider vinegar on page 90, use store-bought vinegar here (since the jars will be water bath canned), or purchase pH strips and perform an acidity test.

1. Thinly slice off the ends of each cucumber and discard. Cut the remaining cucumber into ¼-inch-thick slices and place in a large bowl. Toss with the bell pepper, onion, and salt, cover loosely with a kitchen cloth and set aside at room temperature for 3 to 4 hours, stirring occasionally.

2. Transfer the mixture to a colander. Run cold water over the vegetables and drain.

3. Fill a canner or large stockpot with water, place four or five pint jars inside, and set over medium-high heat. Bring just to the boiling point.

4. Bring the vinegar, brown sugar, mustard seeds, pepper flakes, celery seeds, turmeric, and cloves to a boil in a medium pot. Add the drained vegetable mixture and boil for 3 minutes.

5. Using a jar lifter, remove the hot jars from the canner and place on top of a kitchen cloth on the counter. With the help of a canning funnel, pack the pickles into the jars, reserving ½ inch headspace.

6. Use a spatula or wooden chopstick to remove any trapped air bubbles around the interior circumference of the jars. Wipe the rims clean with a damp cloth. Place on the lids and screw bands, tightening only until fingertip-tight.

7. Again using a jar lifter, slowly place the filled jars in the canner. Be sure that the jars are covered by at least 1 inch of water. Bring to a boil, and then process for 10 minutes, starting the timer once the water is at a full, rolling boil. Adjust for altitude as needed (see page 9 for detailed canning instructions).

BREAD & BUTTER PICKLE GRILLED CHEESE ROUNDS

· AMOUNT VARIES ·

Make as few or as many of these as you'd like. They're great as a snack, a munchie for watching the game, or a cocktail hors d'oeuvre that your guests simply cannot resist.

Sliced sourdough bread

Sharp cheddar cheese

Butter, melted (page 194)

Bread & Butter Pickles

1. Using a 1½-inch round cookie cutter, cut out as many bread rounds as you like.

2. Next, slice some sharp cheddar cheese about ⅛ inch thick. Use the cookie cutter to cut half as many cheese rounds as you have bread rounds. Save the cheese scraps and use in making Pimento Cheese (page 33).

3. Lightly pat the outsides of two bread rounds in the melted butter. Place a cheese round between them. Repeat for as many as you like.

4. Grill in a hot skillet on both sides until the bread is golden and crisp and the cheese is melty.

5. Remove the grilled cheese rounds from the skillet. Gently pry open a corner and place a pickle inside each one. Serve immediately.

PICKLED BEETS

Beets and the South go hand in hand, especially in the cooler regions of the Southern Appalachians where you can harvest beets in both spring and fall. They're imminently versatile, offering a sturdy bulb for all manner of roasting, pickling, and beyond, and leafy greens rich with flavor and nutrition. Despite knowing of their massive health benefits, however, many folks claim to simply not like beets. Which is why pickling them is such a clever means of enjoying their nutrition and their flavor, thanks to the inclusion of a bit of sweetness.

Pickling beets renders them into a truly wonderful condiment. They add brightness and vibrancy to salads, and beauty and tartness to a crudité platter. They're equally delicious whether you eat them straight out of the jar or incorporate them into a dish. Even my young son Huxley couldn't get enough pickled beets when he was beginning his initial foray into solid foods. His face and hands stained a bright crimson, he'd request "More beets, mama! More beets!"

SERVING SUGGESTIONS

- *The tang of pickled beets marries well with the puckery sourness of buttermilk. Purée the two together with a bit of fresh dill to create a buttermilk borscht.*
- *Pile onto a cheeseburger alongside a Green Tomato Pickle (page 50) and melted provolone.*
- *Use as a topping in an arugula and blue cheese salad, with Apple Butter Vinaigrette (page 64). This is one of my all-time favorite salads, especially during the colder months when fresh vegetables are scarce.*

PICKLED BEETS

· MAKES ABOUT 4 PINTS ·

2½ pounds beets

2 cups apple cider vinegar (see Note)

1 cup water

½ cup honey

2 teaspoons pickling salt

2 tablespoons pickling spice blend

1 medium onion, peeled and sliced

NOTE: As per the note about the variable acidity of homemade apple cider vinegar on page 90, use store-bought vinegar here (since the jars will be water bath canned), or purchase pH strips and perform an acidity test.

1. Cut off the stem and root end of the beets. Steam the beets in a steamer basket on the stovetop until tender and easily pierced with a fork, about 15 to 20 minutes. Remove from the heat and set aside briefly to cool. Once they can be handled, cut the beets into wedges.
2. Fill a canner or large stockpot with water, place four or five pint jars inside, and set over medium-high heat. Bring just to the boiling point.
3. Bring the vinegar, water, honey, salt, and pickling spice to a full, rolling boil in a medium pot.

Remove the pot from the heat. Transfer the brine to a pourable, spouted container, such as a heatproof measuring cup, if desired.

4. Using a jar lifter, remove the hot jars from the canner and place on top of a kitchen cloth on the counter. With the help of a canning funnel, pack the beet wedges and onion slices into the jars, topped off by the brine, reserving ½ inch headspace.

5. Use a spatula or wooden chopstick to remove any trapped air bubbles around the interior circumference of the jars. Wipe the rims clean with a damp cloth. Place on the lids and screw bands, tightening only until fingertip-tight.

6. Again using a jar lifter, slowly place the filled jars in the canner. Be sure that the jars are covered by at least 1 inch of water. Bring to a boil, and then process for 25 to 30 minutes, starting the timer once the water is at a full, rolling boil. Adjust for altitude as needed (see page 9 for detailed canning instructions).

PICKLED BEET & FENNEL SALAD

· SERVES 6 TO 8 ·

This is my go-to winter salad. We eat this pretty consistently December through early March. It would also be a welcome addition to your holiday table.

1 pint (2 cups) Pickled Beets

1 cup crumbled blue cheese

¼ cup extra-virgin olive oil

2 fennel bulbs, finely chopped

1 fennel stalk, finely chopped

1. Drain off the beets from the pickling liquid, reserving about ¼ cup of the liquid.
2. In a lidded container, vigorously shake the beet liquid with the blue cheese and olive oil.
3. Place the pickled beets and chopped fennel in a medium mixing bowl. Pour the dressing over and toss to fully combine. Serve immediately.

PICKLED BEET DEVILED EGGS

· MAKES 1 DOZEN ·

Deviled eggs are my Achilles heel, my Kryptonite. I lose most of my self-control in their presence. Must be genetic as my son Huxley shares this tendency. This version, with a bit of pickled beets, horseradish, and tarragon, is as lovely to behold as it is delicious to devour.

1 dozen hard-boiled eggs

3 tablespoons mayonnaise

2 tablespoons extra-virgin olive oil

2 tablespoons Dijon or coarse brown mustard

2 tablespoons chopped tarragon

2 teaspoons prepared horseradish

½ teaspoon sea salt

½ cup Pickled Beets

Fresh chives

1. Cut the eggs in half lengthwise. Remove the yolks and set them aside in a medium mixing bowl.
2. Mix the yolks with the mayonnaise, olive oil, mustard, tarragon, horseradish, and salt until smooth.
3. Fill each egg white half evenly with a small spoonful of the yolk mixture.
4. Slice the beets about ⅛ inch thick. If you're fancy, cut out hearts or any other shape with a small aspic cutter. If you're feeling especially fancy, gently twist holes into the beet hearts with the tip of a bamboo skewer, and pierce them with a 1-inch-long segment of chive stalk, and then top the eggs with the skewered hearts. Otherwise, just top the filled eggs with a little bit of chopped chives and a small piece of pickled beet. Serve immediately, or chill until serving time.

PICKLED OKRA

———

Okra is the unsung hero of the vegetable kingdom. It looks like the Wicked Witch's fingers and has the mucilaginous properties of a slug. But what it lacks in appearance and texture, it more than makes up for in versatility. Fried, sautéed, pickled—okra does it all.

Brought to the United States by way of slave ships, okra has been a part of the culinary canon of the South for centuries. It took root, literally and figuratively, in Southern fields and kitchens soon after being introduced. A member of the mallow family, which also includes cotton, okra thrives in tropical, subtropical, and otherwise warm regions, making the Southeast an ideal growing environment.

I cannot tell you how many people I've met who claim to fiercely loathe okra. However, once they've tried it pickled or fried, they typically sing a different tune (it's also well-loved in gumbos). Just remember to let the pickle sit for several weeks, 1 month ideally, to allow time for the flavors to meld.

SERVING SUGGESTIONS

- *It would be a lovely topping for Serafina's Chicken & Grits (page 141), the sourness balancing out the creaminess of the grits.*
- *Chop into chunky rounds and use as a topping for Pecan Coins (page 165) spread with Pimento Cheese (page 33).*
- *Slice thickly and set out as an ingredient for a Shrimp & Grits Buffet (page 140).*

PICKLED OKRA

· MAKES ABOUT 6 PINTS ·

---

3 cups white vinegar

3 cups water

⅓ cup pickling salt

6 garlic cloves

6 teaspoons dill seeds

3 teaspoons red pepper flakes

2 pounds okra, stem ends trimmed

1. Fill a canner or large stockpot with water, place six or seven pint jars inside, and set over medium-high heat. Bring just to the boiling point.
2. Bring the vinegar, water, and salt to a full, rolling boil in a medium pot. Remove the pot from the heat. Transfer the brine to a pourable, spouted container, such as a heatproof measuring cup, if desired.
3. Using a jar lifter, remove the hot jars from the canner and place on top of a kitchen cloth on the counter. Place 1 garlic clove, 1 teaspoon dill seeds, and ½ teaspoon of the pepper flakes into each jar. With the help of a canning funnel, pack the okra into the jars, topped off by the brine, reserving ½ inch headspace.

4. Use a spatula or wooden chopstick to remove any trapped air bubbles around the interior circumference of the jars. Wipe the rims clean with a damp cloth. Place on the lids and screw bands, tightening only until fingertip-tight.

5. Again using a jar lifter, slowly place the filled jars in the canner. Be sure that the jars are covered by at least 1 inch of water. Bring to a boil, and then process for 10 minutes, starting the timer once the water is at a full, rolling boil. Adjust for altitude as needed (see page 9 for detailed canning instructions).

SPICY BLOODY MARY WITH PICKLED OKRA

· SERVES 1 ·

I didn't think I liked Bloody Marys until I started making my own. What it needed was a bit of pickled okra brine, is all. This recipe makes one cocktail, so if you plan to serve a crowd, scale up accordingly.

3 ounces vodka

6 ounces tomato juice or tomato-based veggie juice

1 tablespoon Pickled Okra brine

1 tablespoon Worcestershire sauce

1 tablespoon lemon juice

½ teaspoon prepared horseradish

Dash of hot sauce

Freshly ground black pepper

Several pinches of celery salt, for the drink and the rim

Lemon slice

Ice, to serve

Celery stalk, for stirring

Pickled Okra, for garnish

1. Mix the vodka, tomato juice, brine, Worcestershire sauce, lemon juice, horseradish, hot sauce, several grinds of pepper, and a pinch of celery salt in a small bowl. Chill in the refrigerator until cool. (If you start with cold tomato juice, the mixture will cool much faster.)

2. Rub the rim of a tall glass with the lemon slice, then dip the rim in a plate of celery salt. Add some ice, leaving plenty of room for the drink.

3. Remove the chilled mixture from the refrigerator. Give it a stir and then pour over the ice. Garnish with a celery stalk and pickled okra, and serve immediately.

SWEET PICKLE RELISH

You'll always find an open jar of sweet pickle relish in my refrigerator, a testament to how frequently I use this condiment. We put it on and in nearly everything, from hot dogs to Spikey Tartar Sauce (page 154) and homemade Russian dressing to potato salad. I make more jars of this relish each summer than any other canned good, except for Canned Tomatoes (page 120).

I imagine my lifelong affinity for this particular condiment can be directly linked to my mother. A fan herself of sweet pickle relish, we always had a jar on hand. It wasn't until my adult years, however, that I tried making it from scratch. Gathering inspiration from my garden's bumper crop of cucumbers, I aspired to recreate the relish of my childhood. It had to be speckled with tiny mustard seeds and bits of red pepper, as well as possess just the right hint of yellow coloring, owing to the presence of turmeric.

I have now been making and serving this relish for a decade, and am deeply satisfied with its versatility. I don't think the South can make exclusive claim on the condiment, but it is certainly used regularly down here. From Virginia to north Florida, the deviled eggs and potato salads and hot dogs of my youth were all redolent with its flavor.

SERVING SUGGESTIONS

- *Deviled eggs are infinitely malleable in their flavor profiles, but my favorite is the classic route: use sweet pickled relish alongside mayonnaise, yellow mustard, and celery seeds as a filling component.*
- *A key component of Spikey Tartar Sauce (page 154), sweet pickle relish expertly offsets the heat and spice of the horseradish.*
- *Pour about ½ cup into a Russet Potato & Dilly Bean Salad (page 42) for an added element of sweetness.*
- *It makes for an iconic and quintessential hot dog topping, alongside Fermented Cabbage (page 116) and celery seeds.*

SWEET PICKLE RELISH

·MAKES ABOUT 6 HALF-PINTS·

4 medium cucumbers, peeled, seeded, and diced

2 to 3 large sweet onions, diced (about 2½ cups)

2 medium green bell peppers, diced (about 1 cup)

2 medium red bell peppers, diced (about 1 cup)

¼ cup pickling or kosher salt

3 cups sugar

2½ cups apple cider vinegar (see Note)

1½ tablespoons yellow mustard seeds

1½ tablespoons celery seeds

1 teaspoon ground turmeric

NOTE: As per the note about the variable acidity of homemade apple cider vinegar on page 90, use store-bought vinegar here (since the jars will be water bath canned), or purchase pH strips and perform an acidity test.

1. Combine the cucumbers, sweet onions, green and red peppers, and salt in a large nonreactive bowl. Toss to combine, cover loosely with a kitchen cloth, and let stand in a cool area for at least four hours or overnight.

2. Drain and rinse the vegetables in a colander. Rinse several times, pressing the vegetables with the back of a wooden spoon to remove all liquid and salty residue. Set aside.

3. In a medium stainless-steel saucepan, combine the sugar, vinegar, mustard seed, celery seed, and turmeric. Add the drained vegetables, and bring the mixture to a boil. Reduce the heat to low, and simmer for 15 minutes.

4. While the relish cooks, fill a canner or large stockpot with water, place 6 half-pint jars inside, and set over medium-high heat. Bring just to the boiling point.

5. Using a jar lifter, remove the hot jars from the canner and place on top of a kitchen cloth on the counter. With the help of a canning funnel, pack the relish into the jars, reserving ½-inch headspace.

6. Use a spatula or wooden chopstick to remove any trapped air bubbles around the interior circumference of the jar. Wipe the rims clean with a damp cloth. Place on the lids and screw bands, tightening only until fingertip-tight.

7. Again using a jar lifter, slowly place the filled jars into the canner. Be sure that there's at least 1 inch of water above the top of the jars. Bring to a boil, and then process for 10 minutes, starting the timer once the water is at a full, rolling boil. Adjust for altitude as needed (see page 9 for detailed canning instructions).

SOUTHERN MACARONI SALAD

· SERVES 6 TO 8 ·

I love mayonnaise as much as the next Southerner (Duke's for life!), but I do not love a macaroni salad adrift in it. This version might seem sacrilegious, given its complete lack of mayonnaise, but trust me: no creamy condiment is needed to buoy this intensely flavorful salad.

---

1 pound elbow noodles

Extra-virgin olive oil

1 half-pint (1 cup) Sweet Pickle Relish

1 large carrot, finely diced

2 stalks celery, finely diced

¼ cup chopped celery leaves

1 teaspoon celery seeds

2 teaspoons sea salt

Freshly ground black pepper

1. Cook the noodles according to package directions, just until al dente. Preheat the oven to 350°F.

2. Drain the noodles in a colander for at least 5 minutes, stirring occasionally to let out the steam.

3. Lightly coat a large rimmed baking sheet with olive oil, and spread out the pasta evenly. Bake for 5 minutes, carefully stir, and then bake for 5 minutes longer. Remove from the oven.

4. Toss the pasta with the relish in a nonreactive bowl or pot. Leave to sit for a few minutes. Stir in the carrot, celery, celery leaves, celery seeds, salt, and several grinds of pepper. Mix until fully combined.

5. Place the bowl in the refrigerator and let it cool for at least 1 hour. Remove from the refrigerator a little before serving to bring it close to room temperature.

PIMENTO CHEESE DIP

· MAKES ABOUT 3 CUPS ·

My husband and I have been making and serving this dip for over a decade. It elicits heaps of praise every time we serve it. Once you've taken to making your own, the store-bought version just won't do. Hoop cheese is a fresh, unripened cheese made only from milk, and no other ingredients. I adore its flavor, but it can be hard to come by. Cheddar cheese makes a fine substitute.

2 pounds hoop or cheddar cheese, cubed

1 cup mayonnaise

½ cup Sweet Pickle Relish

1 tablespoon smoked paprika

Several dashes of hot sauce

½ cup chopped pimento pepper

1 to 2 tablespoons diced pimento pepper, for garnish

1. Combine the cheese, mayonnaise, relish, paprika, and hot sauce in a food processor and process until smooth.
2. Add the chopped pimento and blend just until the pieces are fully incorporated but not puréed.
3. Transfer the mixture to a serving bowl. Top with diced pimento and serve.

SWEET ONION RELISH

If you've spent any time in the southern United States, you've likely encountered Vidalia onions. Named after its place of origin, this sweet onion hails from Vidalia, Georgia, located toward the southeastern part of the state. Their flavor owes to the soil in which they're grown, which contains a low amount of sulfur, producing an onion noticeably sweeter than other varieties.

Sweet onion relish is one of my fifty base recipes for this book on account of its ubiquitous use as a condiment across the South. In roadside stands and farmers' markets throughout the region, jar upon jar of sweet onion relish is readily available for purchase. My guess is that the condiment's prevalence largely stems from the abundance of sweet onions grown here.

I tend to think of this relish as a stealth operative in the culinary landscape. It's not out there shining front and center, in the way that sweet pickle relish does. It's more back-of-the-house operations—just as essential to the success of the mission (this "mission" being a meal on the table) but not taking all the credit.

SERVING SUGGESTIONS

- *Use as a marinade for pork or chicken, as the vinegar in the relish will help tenderize the meat while simultaneously imparting flavor.*
- *This relish would be heavenly mixed into some mayonnaise and liberally spread onto a cheeseburger with Swiss.*
- *Mix with olive oil and white wine vinegar and use as a vinaigrette ingredient.*
- *Layer into a grilled portobello and eggplant sandwich for some sweet and sour punch.*

SWEET ONION RELISH

· MAKES 3 TO 4 HALF-PINTS ·

4 cups chopped sweet onions, such as Vidalia
(about 4 onions)

2 teaspoons pickling salt

½ cup sugar

1 cup red wine vinegar

1 teaspoon dried thyme, or 1 tablespoon
minced fresh thyme

2 garlic cloves, minced

Zest of 1 orange

1. Place 2 cups of the onions in a medium nonreactive mixing bowl. Sprinkle 1 teaspoon of the salt over them. Cover with the remaining 2 cups onions, followed by the remaining 1 teaspoon salt. Stir with a wooden spoon, cover loosely with a kitchen cloth, and set aside at room temperature for 4 hours.
2. Drain the onions in a colander, pressing on them with a wooden or metal spoon. Don't rinse with water, though, just press out and discard any juices. Set aside.
3. Fill a canner or large stockpot with water, place three or four half-pint jars inside, and set over medium-high heat. Bring just to the boiling point while preparing the relish.

4. Combine the sugar, vinegar, thyme, garlic, and orange zest in a medium pot. Heat gradually over medium-low until the sugar is completely dissolved. Increase the heat to medium-high and bring to a boil.

5. Add the onions to the pot. Stir to fully combine, reduce the heat to low, and simmer gently for 10 minutes. Remove the pot from the heat.

6. Using a jar lifter, remove the hot jars from the canner and place on top of a kitchen cloth on the counter. With the help of a canning funnel, pack the onion relish into the jars, reserving ½ inch headspace.

7. Use a spatula or wooden chopstick to remove any trapped air bubbles around the interior circumference of the jars. Wipe the rims clean with a damp cloth. Place on the lids and screw bands, tightening only until fingertip-tight.

8. Again using a jar lifter, slowly place the filled jars in the canner. Be sure that the jars are covered by at least 1 inch of water. Bring to a boil, and then process 15 minutes, starting the timer once the water is at a full, rolling boil. Adjust for altitude as needed (see page 9 for detailed canning instructions).

GOAT CHEESE & ONION RELISH SPREAD

· MAKES ABOUT 2 CUPS ·

It's easy to find countless uses for this delicious spread. I'm particularly fond of spreading it on a cracker with a little Bourbon Bacon Jam (page 178) on top. It would also be a delicious grilled cheese sandwich filling.

1 half-pint (1 cup) Sweet Onion Relish

8 ounces goat cheese, room temperature

8 ounces Cream Cheese, room temperature (page 202)

1. Empty the jar of onion relish, brine and all, into a medium mixing bowl.

2. Add the goat cheese and cream cheese, and stir until fully incorporated. Serve immediately, or chill in the refrigerator and bring out about 15 minutes before serving.

HOT DOG SHRIMP ROLLS WITH ONION RELISH

· SERVES 8 ·

How do you satisfy a lobster roll craving in a part of the country with hardly any lobster? I give you the shrimp roll. Just as tender and delicious, and sourced much closer to home, it's one of our favorite foods to eat when fresh shrimp is in season.

8 hot dogs

1 tablespoon Bacon Drippings (page 176)

1 pound shrimp, peeled, deveined, and cooked

¼ cup mayonnaise

¼ cup Sweet Onion Relish plus additional
   to serve

1 stalk celery, finely diced

2 tablespoons prepared mustard

1 tablespoon smoked paprika

1 teaspoon celery seeds

Pinch of sea salt

8 hot dog buns, lightly toasted

1. Using a pointy tip knife, split the hot dogs lengthwise, not quite all the way through.
2. Warm the bacon drippings in a skillet or saucepan over medium heat. Add the hot dogs and cook until nicely browned and cooked through. Remove the pan from the heat.
3. Combine the shrimp with the mayonnaise, relish, celery, mustard, paprika, celery seeds, and salt in a medium mixing bowl. Stir to fully combine.
4. Put a hot dog and a few tablespoons of the shrimp mixture into each bun. Top with a little extra relish. Serve immediately.

DILLY BEANS

If you have ever grown green beans, you know just how prolific they can be. Though one can pressure can and freeze them, my favorite means of preserving the bean bounty is by pickling. Dilly beans are a delicious at-the-ready snack, especially lovely when partnered with a wedge of sharp cheese.

The history of how dill became so prevalent in pickle-making is a bit murky. Found wild in southern Russia, the Mediterranean region, and western Africa, dill found its way into the cuisines of those regions, and was widely used by the ancient Greeks and Romans. Eastern European immigrants were likely responsible for bringing the herb to the New World. Loving an abundance of sunshine and requiring a warm environment, dill found a welcome home in the soils of the southeastern United States.

Growing up, my mother always kept a jar of dried dill in her pantry. She'd sprinkle it on meatballs and sometimes in potato salad. Dilly beans weren't something she regularly made, nor did she offer them at our dinner table. I came across the pickle all the time as a child, but it wasn't until adulthood that I had an opportunity to sample them. I was smitten at first bite, and have been growing green beans and dill in my garden for years now with the sole purpose of putting up pints each summer.

SERVING SUGGESTIONS

- *Pickles, unsurprisingly, pair well with other pickles. Set out as a component of a crudité platter.*
- *Use it to garnish a Spicy Bloody Mary with Pickled Okra (page 29) for an even greater contrast to the spiciness of the drink.*
- *Chop into bite-sized pieces and scatter over a bagel covered with Cream Cheese (page 202) and lox or Bacon (page 176).*

DILLY BEANS

· MAKES ABOUT 5 PINTS ·

---

2 pounds green beans	5 teaspoons dill seeds
3 cups white vinegar	5 teaspoons brown mustard seeds
3 cups water	2½ teaspoons black peppercorns
¼ cup pickling salt	10 sprigs fresh dill
10 garlic cloves, peeled	

1. Fill a canner or large stockpot with water, place five pint jars inside, and set over medium-high heat. Bring just to the boiling point.
2. Bring the vinegar, water, and salt to a full, rolling boil in a medium pot. Remove the pot from the heat. Transfer the brine to a pourable, spouted container, such as a heatproof measuring cup, if desired.

3. Using a jar lifter, remove the hot jars from the canner and place on top of a kitchen cloth on the counter. Place 2 garlic cloves, 1 teaspoon dill seeds, 1 teaspoon mustard seeds, ½ teaspoon peppercorns, and 2 sprigs fresh dill in each jar. With the help of a canning funnel, pack the green beans into the jars, topped off by the brine, reserving ½ inch headspace.

4. Use a spatula or wooden chopstick to remove any trapped air bubbles around the interior circumference of the jars. Wipe the rims clean with a damp cloth. Place on the lids and screw bands, tightening only until fingertip-tight.

5. Again using a jar lifter, slowly place the filled jars in the canner. Be sure that the jars are covered by at least 1 inch of water. Bring to a boil, and then process for 10 minutes, starting the timer once the water is at a full, rolling boil. Adjust for altitude as needed (see page 9 for detailed canning instructions).

SOUTHERN PROSCIUTTO-WRAPPED DILLY BEANS

· MAKES ABOUT 1 DOZEN ·

Welcome to your new favorite thing. Once the pickles are ready, wrap them in a bed of goat cheese and prosciutto. Excellent with a glass of jammy red zinfandel.

4 ounces goat cheese, room temperature	A few stalks of celery
2 tablespoons capers	One 4-ounce package prosciutto
¼ cup sun-dried tomatoes, finely chopped	1 pint (2 cups) Dilly Beans

1. Combine the goat cheese with the capers and sun-dried tomatoes in a medium mixing bowl.

2. Cut the celery into 3-inch-long sticks. Spread about 2 teaspoons of the cheese mixture on the inside of a stick of celery.

3. Press a dilly bean into it and wrap the whole thing up with a piece of prosciutto.

4. Repeat the process until you run out. Serve immediately, or chill in the refrigerator and bring out 10 minutes before serving.

RUSSET POTATO & DILLY BEAN SALAD

· SERVES 8 TO 10 ·

I grew up with my mother's potato salad. Packed with mayonnaise, yellow mustard, and hard-boiled eggs, it was delicious. This potato salad is nothing like it. With all due respect to my mom, I like a bit of acid in my potato salad to cut through all that creaminess. That is achieved here threefold: via apple cider vinegar, dilly beans, and their brine. I could eat this potato salad as a meal, it's that good.

¼ cup Apple Cider Vinegar (page 88)

2 tablespoons sea salt for the cooking water

4 pounds russet potatoes, peeled and cut into bite-size cubes

1 cup Dilly Beans, chopped to ¾-inch lengths

½ cup Dilly Bean brine

1 cup mayonnaise

2 tablespoons coarse prepared mustard

Sea salt and freshly ground black pepper

1. Stir the vinegar and salt into 3 quarts of water in a large pot. Add the potatoes and turn the heat to high. As soon as the water comes to a boil, turn the temperature down to simmer. Cook for 10 minutes, stirring occasionally.

2. Preheat the oven to 350°F.

3. When the potatoes are done, drain them well in a colander and let them sit for 5 minutes to let off some steam.

4. Spread out the potatoes on a large rimmed baking sheet. Bake for 10 minutes. Remove the pan from the oven and let cool for about 10 minutes.

5. Transfer the potatoes to a medium mixing bowl. Gently fold in the dilly beans, pickling brine, mayonnaise, mustard, and salt and pepper to taste.

6. Cover the mixing bowl and place in the refrigerator. Cool at least 1 hour before serving.

DILL PICKLES

Before the advent of refrigeration, cultures across the globe utilized a wide range of food preservation techniques—from salting to drying, from root cellaring to rendering into beverages—to extend the edible life of fruits and vegetables. Pickling is one such low-fi technique, using either salt water or vinegar to keep pathogens and inhospitable organisms from spoiling food before it is consumed. My recipe for dill pickles uses vinegar as the preserving solution.

Snacking on whole dill pickles has been a familial lifetime pastime. Mom was a devoted fan of all products of the Mt. Olive brand, based in Mount Olive, North Carolina. The largest independent pickle company in the United States, and the best-selling pickle brand in the Southeast, we were never without a jar, or five, of Mt. Olive's offerings in our pantry and refrigerator.

Inspired as a child watching my grandmother Nanny produce countless jars of canned goods, I knew that dill pickles would assuredly be a go-to in my own kitchen as an adult. Dill pickles aren't just for pregnant ladies. They're for kids, adults, and seniors alike, anyone desirous of a puckery bite of something. My garden yields basketfuls of pickling cucumbers all summer long, and this is my most frequent means of using them up.

SERVING SUGGESTIONS

- *The tang of pickles is an excellent complement to the mild flavor of grilled cheese. Slice lengthwise and use as a component in your favorite grilled cheese sandwich.*
- *Make a dirty martini with pickle slivers and a splash of the brine, too.*
- *Chop into small pieces and use alongside capers and minced fresh dill in tuna or salmon salad.*

DILL PICKLES

· MAKES ABOUT 8 PINTS ·

---

6 pounds pickling cucumbers	8 garlic cloves, peeled
¾ cup pickling salt	4 teaspoons dill seeds
4 cups white vinegar	8 fresh dill sprigs, or 4 teaspoons dried dill
3½ cups water	Black peppercorns

1. Rinse the cucumbers in cold water. Cut a thin slice off the blossom end of each cucumber. If you can't tell which end is the blossom end, just remove a thin slice from each end. Discard or compost the ends.
2. Place the cucumbers in a large nonreactive bowl, such as glass or ceramic. Add ½ cup of the salt, cover with water, stir to combine, and cover loosely with a kitchen cloth. Place the bowl in the refrigerator to cool for at least 8 hours.

3. Drain the cucumbers and rinse them well under cold water. At this point, you may leave them whole, halve them, or cut them into quarters. Set aside.

4. Fill a canner or large stockpot with water, place eight pint jars inside, and set over medium-high heat. Bring just to the boiling point.

5. Bring the vinegar, water, and the remaining ¼ cup salt to a boil in a medium pot. Reduce the heat to low, and simmer gently for 5 minutes. Remove the pot from the heat. Transfer the brine to a pourable, spouted container, such as a heatproof measuring cup, if desired.

6. Using a jar lifter, remove the hot jars from the canner and place on top of a kitchen cloth on the counter. Place 1 garlic clove, ½ teaspoon dill seeds, 1 fresh dill sprig or ½ teaspoon dried dill, and 8 peppercorns in each jar. With the help of a canning funnel, pack the reserved cucumbers into the jars, topped off by the brine, reserving ½ inch headspace.

7. Use a spatula or wooden chopstick to remove any trapped air bubbles around the interior circumference of the jars. Wipe the rims clean with a damp cloth. Place on the lids and screw bands, tightening only until fingertip-tight.

8. Again using a jar lifter, slowly place the filled jars in the canner. Be sure that the jars are covered by at least 1 inch of water. Bring to a boil, and then process for 10 minutes, starting the timer once the water is at a full, rolling boil. Adjust for altitude as needed (see page 9 for detailed canning instructions).

FRIED DILL PICKLES WITH SORGHUM MAYO

· AMOUNT VARIES ·

I came late to fried dill pickles. They just sounded too awful to stomach. And then I came across a cornmeal-battered version and it all came together for me. Don't skip the sorghum mayo! It complements the pickles profoundly.

½ cup all-purpose flour	Dash of hot sauce
½ cup medium-grind cornmeal (see Note)	1 pint (2 cups) Dill Pickles, cut into ¼-inch chips
1 teaspoon granulated garlic	Peanut oil for frying
1 teaspoon sea salt	¼ cup mayonnaise
1 egg, beaten	1 teaspoon sorghum syrup

NOTE: Fine-grind cornmeal is also okay if you don't prefer the crunchiness.

1. Combine the flour, cornmeal, garlic, and salt in a medium mixing bowl.
2. Whisk a dash of hot sauce into the egg.
3. Dab the pickle slices on a paper towel or kitchen cloth to remove excess moisture.
4. Dip the pickle slices in the egg and then dredge them in the cornmeal mixture. Place on a large plate or platter and set them aside.
5. Heat ½ inch of peanut oil in a large cast iron skillet to 360°F. Carefully lay half of the battered pickles in the pan. Cook 90 seconds per side, until golden brown.

6. Using a kitchen spider or slotted spoon, remove the pickles from the pan. Drain on a paper towel, and then repeat with the second half.

7. Stir the sorghum into the mayonnaise, creating the dipping sauce.

8. Be sure to let the fried pickles cool for a few minutes before serving, as the pickle juices can be very hot. Serve with the sorghum mayonnaise.

POTATO PICKLE SOUP

· SERVES 6 TO 8 ·

Stay with me on this one. I know it sounds weird. I really do. But it is so, so very good. Creamy, rich potato soup is deeply balanced by dill pickle chunks. Just the thing to fill you up on a gray, rainy day.

---

2 pounds russet potatoes	2 carrots, diced
1 cup heavy cream	6 cups Chicken Stock (page 187)
2 tablespoons Butter (page 194)	1 teaspoon sea salt
3 strips Bacon (page 176)	1 pint (2 cups) Dill Pickles, diced
1 medium onion, diced	3 ounces grated cheese, to serve (optional)

1. Preheat the oven to 400°F. Place the potatoes on a large rimmed baking sheet. Pierce each one several times with a fork. Bake for 45 minutes, until tender. Remove from the oven and let the potatoes cool.

2. Once cool enough to handle, peel the potato skins from the flesh. Discard or compost the skins. Place the flesh in a medium mixing bowl, add the cream and butter, and mash until smooth and fully combined.

3. Cook the bacon in a large pot or Dutch oven over medium heat until it starts to get crispy, about 7 to 9 minutes. Remove the bacon from the pan and set it aside to drain on a paper towel.

4. Add the onion and carrots to the bacon grease left behind in the pot and cook for 5 minutes. Pour in the stock and bring to a boil. Reduce the heat to a simmer and stir in the mashed potatoes and salt.

5. Remove the pot from the heat. Using an immersion blender, purée the soup in the pot until smooth (or transfer to a food processor and purée in batches).

6. Return the pot to the stovetop and simmer over low heat for 30 minutes, stirring frequently and scraping the bottom to keep it from sticking.

7. Stir in the pickles and cook for 5 more minutes.

8. Crumble the bacon and serve with the soup as a garnish, along with grated cheese, if using.

PICKLED WATERMELON RIND

Originating in southern Africa, watermelons have made their way around the globe many times over. The watery, ruby-hued fruit was introduced to the New World by way of European colonists and African slaves, and rapidly spread across the country. Native Americans began cultivating watermelons across the southern United States in the seventeenth century. These days, many U.S. states grow the fruit commercially.

Though it's most common to consume the flesh of watermelons, people have pickled the rind for centuries in this country. Civil war documents even mention directions on how to pickle watermelon rind. Rind pickling has long been practiced in parts of Europe, most notably in Germany, as well as in Russia. Times of food scarcity, coupled with a European inclination to pickle most everything, likely served as the impetus for watermelon rind pickling in the southern United States.

I didn't grow up eating pickled watermelon rind, but I've long been aware of it. When I decided to try making my own. I was surprised by how much I liked it and how much it reminded me of the flavors of Christmas—sugar and spice. Be forewarned: it is decidedly sweet, almost candy-like, for a pickle. That said, it is exceptionally delicious, and beyond easy to fish out with your fingers and eat straight from the jar.

SERVING SUGGESTIONS

- *The spices used in my pickled watermelon rind are flavors also associated with holiday baking. To that end, place a single cube onto a Saltine (page 85) spread liberally with Cream Cheese (page 202) for a holiday hors d'oeuvre.*
- *Chop into small pieces and scatter over a romaine and goat cheese salad.*
- *Mince, mix with mayonnaise, and spread onto a toasted Kaiser roll, then top with roast beef.*

PICKLED WATERMELON RIND

· MAKES ABOUT 3 PINTS ·

---

6 cups water

½ cup pickling salt

6 cups peeled 1-inch watermelon rind cubes

1½ cups white vinegar

2 cups sugar

2 teaspoons whole cloves

2 teaspoons whole allspice

Three 2-inch cinnamon sticks, broken in half

2 teaspoons black peppercorns

1. Place the water and salt in a large nonreactive bowl, such as glass or ceramic. Stir until the salt has fully dissolved. Add the watermelon cubes and stir to combine. Cover the bowl loosely with a kitchen cloth, and set aside at room temperature for 8 to 12 hours.
2. Transfer the mixture to a colander. Run cold water over the watermelon rind and drain.
3. Fill a canner or large stockpot with water, place three or four pint jars inside, and set over medium-high heat. Bring just to the boiling point.

4. Bring the vinegar, sugar, cloves, allspice, cinnamon, and peppercorns to a boil in a medium pot. Add the watermelon rind, and boil for 8 minutes.

5. Using a jar lifter, remove the hot jars from the canner and place on top of a kitchen cloth on the counter. With the help of a canning funnel, pack the pickles into the jars, reserving ½ inch headspace.

6. Use a spatula or wooden chopstick to remove any trapped air bubbles around the interior circumference of the jars. Wipe the rims clean with a damp cloth. Place on the lids and screw bands, tightening only until fingertip-tight.

7. Again using a jar lifter, slowly place the filled jars in the canner. Be sure that the jars are covered by at least 1 inch of water. Bring to a boil, and then process for 10 minutes, starting the timer once the water is at a full, rolling boil. Adjust for altitude as needed (see page 9 for detailed canning instructions).

WATERMELON RIND SLOPPY JOES

· SERVES 4 TO 6 ·

When considering uses for watermelon rind that exceed simply eating chunks whole, I kept returning to its flavor profile. Cinnamon, cloves, allspice. Then it dawned on me—that's the same flavor profile of sloppy Joes. Hence, this unlikely pairing was brought to life. It works in all the right ways, and then some.

1 pound ground beef	1 cup Ketchup (page 110)
2 tablespoons extra-virgin olive oil	1 tablespoon Worcestershire sauce
1 medium onion, diced	Freshly ground black pepper
1 red, yellow, or orange bell pepper, diced	Sea salt
1 pint (2 cups) Pickled Watermelon Rind	Hamburger buns, lightly toasted

1. Warm a large saucepan over medium-high heat. Add the beef and brown for 6 to 8 minutes, until cooked through. Remove the pan from the heat. Place a mesh sieve or colander over a bowl. Pour in the beef and drain off the juices. Discard the juices (or give them to your dog!).

2. Return the pan to the stovetop and warm over medium heat. Add the olive oil, onion, and bell pepper, and sauté for 10 minutes, until the vegetables are browned around the edges.

3. Chop the pickled watermelon rind into a fine relish-like consistency. Add the watermelon, beef, ketchup, Worcestershire, and several grinds of pepper to the pan with the vegetables. Stir to combine.

4. Bring to a simmer, turn the heat to low, and simmer for 10 to 15 minutes, until the sauce thickens a bit. Add salt to taste, a little bit at a time, until the salty-sweet balance is right for you. Serve between hamburger buns.

GREEN TOMATO PICKLES

———

Pickling was brought to the New World by colonists, who in turn introduced the practice to the Native Americans. The Cherokee, in particular, were especially drawn to pickling, having learned it from German settlers in the Southern Appalachian region. As the area was producing tomatoes in abundance, it only stands to reason that pickling the unripened fruits toward the end of harvest season would occur.

From there, the idea blossomed to cover the pickles in cornmeal and fry them, rendering the pickles into fried green tomatoes. Fried green tomatoes are now as ubiquitous across the Southeast as bourbon, bacon, and barbeque. I have been enjoying them my entire life, but came to love them in a more personal way after viewing (many, many times) the 1991 film *Fried Green Tomatoes*, based on the Fannie Flagg novel.

Though you may be tempted to wallow in despair at the sight of unripened tomatoes in your garden at the end of summer, I encourage you to rejoice instead! You are in the possession of precious emeralds, eagerly waiting to be rendered into pickles (or, at least that's what I tell myself). Green tomato pickles are a bright light in my pantry, at all times of the year, but especially during the colder months, when they serve as a silent reminder of the cycles of growth and change.

SERVING SUGGESTIONS

- *The sourness of green tomato pickles pairs perfectly with the smoky saltiness of bacon. Incorporate a slice or two into a BLGT sandwich (Bacon, page 176).*
- *Beat an egg, dip a green tomato pickle in it, then dip in medium-grind cornmeal and fry in peanut oil. Serve with Comeback Sauce (page 108).*
- *Chop finely and stuff in pork tacos.*

GREEN TOMATO PICKLES

· MAKES ABOUT 4 PINTS ·

1½ cups apple cider vinegar (see Note)

1½ cups water

2 tablespoons pickling salt

4 teaspoons celery seeds

4 teaspoons dill seeds

4 garlic cloves, peeled

2 teaspoons yellow mustard seeds

2 teaspoons whole cloves

3 pounds firm green tomatoes, sliced

NOTE: As per the note about the variable acidity of homemade apple cider vinegar on page 88, use store-bought vinegar here (since the jars will be water bath canned), or purchase pH strips and perform an acidity test.

1. Fill a canner or large stockpot with water, place four or five pint jars inside, and set over medium-high heat. Bring just to the boiling point.
2. Bring the vinegar, water, and salt to a full, rolling boil in a medium pot. Remove the pot from the heat. Transfer the brine to a pourable, spouted container, such as a heatproof measuring cup, if desired.
3. Using a jar lifter, remove the hot jars from the canner and place on top of a kitchen cloth on the counter. Place 1 teaspoon celery seeds, 1 teaspoon dill seeds, 1 garlic clove, ½ teaspoon mustard seeds, and ½ teaspoon whole cloves into each jar. With the help of a canning funnel, pack the green tomatoes into the jars, topped off by the brine, reserving ½ inch headspace.
4. Use a spatula or wooden chopstick to remove any trapped air bubbles around the interior circumference of the jars. Wipe the rims clean with a damp cloth. Place on the lids and screw bands, tightening only until fingertip-tight.
5. Again using a jar lifter, slowly place the filled jars in the canner. Be sure that the jars are covered by at least 1 inch of water. Bring to a boil, and then process for 10 minutes, starting the timer once the water is at a full, rolling boil. Adjust for altitude as needed (see page 9 for detailed canning instructions).

CHEESE CRISPS WITH GREEN TOMATO PICKLES

· MAKES 18 TO 24 ·

Make these when you want a snack but you're not sure what. They cover all the flavor bases—salty, creamy, crisp, and tangy at once—so you're bound to end up satisfying any craving.

8 ounces cheddar cheese	1 pint (2 cups) Green Tomato Pickles
¼ cup all-purpose flour	3 ounces country ham, cooked and chopped
Olive oil for frying	Freshly ground black pepper

1. Grate the cheese into a medium mixing bowl. Add the flour and stir to coat the cheese evenly.
2. Form tight golf ball–size mounds out of the cheese.
3. Lightly coat a cast iron skillet with olive oil and set over medium-high heat. Flatten the cheese balls into thin pancakes.
4. Fry the pancakes in the heated pan until deep golden brown and crispy—about 3 to 4 minutes on each side. Remove from the pan and drain on paper towels. Repeat with the remaining cheese mounds until all are cooked, adding a small amount of olive oil to the pan with each batch.
5. Top each cheese crisp with a green tomato pickle slice, a little country ham, and several grinds of pepper. Cut into wedges (a pizza wheel is helpful for this task) and serve immediately.

SPICED PICKLED PEACHES

Is any Southern fruit finer than a ripe peach on a scorching summer's day? The relief and joy offered is incomparable. A member of the rose family, which includes almonds, cherries, apricots, and plums, peaches have been cultivated in China for thousands of years, and slowly made their way west. Thomas Jefferson maintained peach trees at Monticello, but commercial peach production in the United States didn't take off until the 1800s.

Although Georgia dominated the peach market after the Civil War—and is the state most folks think of when they imagine the provenance of Southern peaches—South Carolina has produced more peaches than the "Peach State" since the 1950s. There is a good deal of rivalry between the two states as to where the tastier peaches grow. Nonetheless, these days, California produces far more peaches than South Carolina and Georgia combined.

I wait all year for peaches to come into season, and don't purchase them until they do. In my estimation, fewer disappointments in life are as profound as biting into a mealy peach. When ripe, though, peaches can be downright rhapsodic. Those are the peaches you want when making these pickles—aromatic, with a bit of give when gently pushed.

SERVING SUGGESTIONS

- *Ham and peaches are a classic Southern foods pairing, their saltiness and sweetness playing off each other. Add some spiced pickled peaches to a ham sandwich or pass around a bowl of spiced pickled peaches alongside a platter of sliced sweet ham.*
- *Chop into bite-size pieces, and use as a Hoecake (page 123) topping, served with crumbled feta or goat cheese.*
- *Slow cook with a whole chicken and serve over Grits (page 138).*

SPICED PICKLED PEACHES

· MAKES ABOUT 4 PINTS ·

---

3 pounds peaches

2 cups white vinegar

1½ cups water

½ cup honey

Three 2-inch cinnamon sticks, broken in half

2 teaspoons whole cloves

1 teaspoon whole allspice

1. Using a pointy tip knife, make a small crosshatch score across the bottom of each peach. Fill a large metal bowl with ice water, and place it in the sink.
2. Bring a large pot of water to a boil over high heat. Drop the peaches into the boiling water for 30 to 60 seconds, until their skins split. Using a slotted spoon, remove the peaches from the pot and drop them into the reserved ice water bath. Once they are cool enough to handle, slip off their skins, cut them in half, and discard or compost the pits.
3. Fill a canner or large stockpot with water, place four pint jars inside, and set over medium-high heat. Bring just to the boiling point.

4. Combine the vinegar, water, honey, cinnamon, cloves, and allspice in a medium saucepan over medium heat until the honey has fully dissolved. Raise the heat to high, and boil for 5 minutes. Remove the pan from the heat.

5. Using a jar lifter, remove the hot jars from the canner and place on top of a kitchen cloth on the counter. With the help of a canning funnel, pack peaches into each jar, and then pour the spice brine on top, reserving ½ inch headspace and making sure some spices are included in each jar.

6. Use a spatula or wooden chopstick to remove any trapped air bubbles around the interior circumference of the jars. Wipe the rims clean with a damp cloth. Place on the lids and screw bands, tightening only until fingertip-tight.

7. Again using a jar lifter, slowly place the filled jars in the canner. Be sure that the jars are covered by at least 1 inch of water. Bring to a boil, and then process for 15 minutes, starting the timer once the water is at a full, rolling boil. Adjust for altitude as needed (see page 12 for detailed canning instructions).

PICKLED PEACH SALSA

· MAKES ABOUT 2 CUPS ·

This is a great throw-together salsa when fresh fruit isn't in season or on hand. It's delicious with fish tacos, as well as served alongside scrambled eggs.

---

1 pint (2 cups) Spiced Pickled Peaches

1 (4-ounce) can chopped green chilies

1 cup chopped cilantro

1 tablespoon extra-virgin olive oil

1 teaspoon dried oregano

½ teaspoon ground cumin

Pinch of sea salt

1. Drain the peaches and remove all the whole spices.

2. Pat the peaches dry on a kitchen cloth or paper towel.

3. Chop the peaches to a salsa consistency and place in a medium nonreactive bowl.

4. Add the chilies, cilantro, olive oil, oregano, cumin, and salt. Stir to fully combine.

5. Let the salsa sit for at least 10 minutes before serving to allow the flavors to meld. Serve with fish, chicken, pork chops, or fried eggs.

PICKLED EGGS

———

Though many folks know of pickled eggs, fewer have dared to sample them. I'd wager to guess this is because they are most commonly viewed in rural Southern gas stations or dive bars of unknown repute. That they tend to be suspended in what appears to be a vat of suspicious red liquid only adds to their off-putting nature.

Well, I'm here to help you put all those images and associations behind you and move toward a full embrace of pickled eggs. They're just far too delicious to be left out of your culinary repertoire. Brought to the New World by the British, who have long offered pickled eggs in their public houses and taverns, these preserved eggs couldn't be easier to make.

From late spring until about August, I find myself flush with chicken eggs. We keep a flock of laying hens, and they go into heavy production when daylight hours exceed those of darkness. When I've had as many cooked egg variations as I want and still find myself with eggs to spare, I turn to pickling. An excellent snack as well as a stellar ingredient for incorporating into dishes, pickled eggs are always welcome in my kitchen.

SERVING SUGGESTIONS

- *The tang of pickled eggs partners quite well with the creamy bite of Caesar salad dressing. Scatter slices over a Caesar salad, and then top with crumbled Bacon (page 176).*
- *These hand-held foods are delicious eaten outside, on a summer day, paired with a nice pilsner.*
- *Chop into bite-size pieces and use as a component in egg salad, alongside fresh tarragon, mayonnaise, and a bit of Dijon mustard.*

———

PICKLED EGGS

· MAKES 1 DOZEN ·

———

3 cups water	1 tablespoon black peppercorns
1 cup Apple Cider Vinegar (page 88)	2 teaspoons sea salt
2 garlic cloves, sliced	3 or 4 fresh thyme sprigs
1 tablespoon honey	1 dozen hard-boiled eggs, shelled

1. Bring the water, vinegar, garlic, honey, peppercorns, salt, and thyme to boil in a medium pot. Reduce the heat to low and simmer for 20 minutes.
2. Remove the pot from heat, cover, and leave until completely cool.
3. Place the eggs in a lidded container (a glass hinge-top canister works well) and pour the cooled brine over the eggs.
4. Keep the eggs chilled in the refrigerator until serving time. They are best when eaten within 7 days.

SCOTCH PICKLED EGGS

· MAKES ABOUT 1 DOZEN ·

I have been in love with Scotch eggs since taking my first bite at Jack of the Wood, a brewery and pub in downtown Asheville, North Carolina. My son was an infant at the time, and had generously decided to take a deep, lengthy nap while my husband and I stopped in for lunch. The description of fried sausage wrapped around a hard-boiled egg was too good to pass up, and am I ever glad I didn't. Since then, I've ordered them whenever I see them on a menu. As I was thinking of uses for pickled eggs, Scotch eggs came to mind. I'd never heard of a pickled Scotch egg, but that didn't stop me from trying. Opting for egg slivers with a dab of grainy mustard instead of whole eggs, these Scotch eggs are heavy on flavor without being overwhelming.

4 Pickled Eggs

1 pound Breakfast Sausage (page 182)

3 teaspoons grainy prepared mustard

1½ cups fresh breadcrumbs

1 teaspoon sea salt

Freshly ground black pepper

1 egg, beaten

Peanut oil for frying

1. Slice the pickled eggs into round slices with an egg slicer, or about ¼ inch thick.
2. Form the sausage into ping pong–size balls, and then press into thin patties.
3. Put a dab of mustard (about ¼ teaspoon) in between two slices of egg, then center that between two sausage patties. Pinch the sausage together around the sides of the egg pieces, enclosing the egg slices fully. Repeat until you run out of sausage.
4. Combine the breadcrumbs with the salt and several grinds of pepper in a small bowl. Dunk the sausage and egg patties in the beaten egg, shake off any excess, and then dredge the patties in the breadcrumb mixture. Place the patties on a large plate or platter.
5. Pour around ½ inch peanut oil into a large cast iron skillet. Heat the oil to about 370°F. Add half the Scotch eggs, turning the heat up slightly after adding them to the pan to bring the temperature of the oil back up.
6. Pan-fry for about 2 minutes per side, until golden brown and cooked through.
7. Remove the Scotch eggs from the pan using a kitchen spider or slotted spoon. Set aside to drain on a paper towel, and repeat until you have fried all the patties. Serve immediately.

PARIS OF THE SOUTH SALAD

· SERVES 4 ·

Asheville, North Carolina, has long been referred to as the "Paris of the South," owing to its unique, eclectic feel, large presence of artists, Art Deco architecture, and bohemian, relaxed vibe. I was thinking of a niçoise salad—a salad hailing from the South of France that often includes tuna, green beans, and hard-boiled eggs—when I realized that using my town's moniker was the perfect solution for what I had in mind. Swapping in some pickled eggs, dilly beans, smoked mountain trout, and, naturally, a bit of bacon brought this European delight into the Blue Ridge Mountains.

2 strips Bacon (page 176)

½ pound new potatoes, cut into large bite-size pieces

1 cup Chicken Stock (page 187)

Pinch of sea salt for the potatoes

8 ounces lettuce, leaves torn

5 ounces smoked trout

20 Dilly Beans (page 38)

1 tomato, sliced into thin wedges

4 Pickled Eggs, cut into wedges or sliced with an egg slicer

FOR THE VINAIGRETTE

¼ cup Sweet Onion Relish (page 35)

¼ cup extra-virgin olive oil

1 tablespoon prepared mustard

1 teaspoon granulated garlic

1 teaspoon sea salt

Freshly ground black pepper

1. Cook the bacon in a cast iron skillet until lightly crispy. Remove the bacon and drain on a paper towel, leaving the grease in the pan. Cool the bacon slightly, and then chop into small pieces.

2. Add the potatoes to the bacon grease and sauté for 5 minutes over medium heat.

3. Add the chicken stock to the pan, reduce the heat to low, and simmer for 15 minutes, until the liquid has cooked off. Remove the pan from the heat and gently toss the potatoes with a pinch of salt. Set aside.

4. Make the vinaigrette. Blend the relish, olive oil, mustard, garlic, salt, and several grinds of pepper in a food processor or blender until emulsified.

5. Combine the lettuce, trout, dilly beans, tomatoes, bacon, potatoes, and vinaigrette in a large bowl. Gently toss until everything is fully coated with the vinaigrette.

6. Plate the salads, then top with the pickled eggs and some extra pepper, if desired. Serve immediately.

2

JAMS
— & —
SPREADS

APPLE BUTTER

————

I once jokingly wrote that if my family were to ever have a family mascot, it should be an apple. To say that we are apple people is to say that water is wet. My great-grandmother, grandmother, and mother truly, sincerely loved, and continue to love, all things apple. When you consider the history of apples in the Southern Appalachians, this intense love is really not surprising.

At one point, over a thousand apple varieties grew in the Southern and Central Appalachians, writes author Ronni Lundy in her cookbook *Victuals*. The primary reason that colonists brought apple trees to the New World was to produce fresh and hard cider for drinking. North Carolina, the state I've called home for over half of my life, is currently the seventh largest apple producer in the United States. With access to so many varieties grown in the area, it stands to reason I'd develop a lifelong affinity for the fruit.

I have eaten apple butter my entire life. My brother, mother, and I are all fierce devotees, our love of it introduced to us from my grandmother, and she in turn by her own mother. When I began outlining what pantry staples I deemed essential for this book, it was one of the first I wrote down. I think everyone in the South is familiar with apple butter, where it is regularly served in Southern restaurants, put down on the table with complimentary biscuits and butter.

Over the past decade, it has become my go-to holiday gift, handed out to family in person or via snail mail. Fresh apple cider instead of water is my secret for a sweet, but not overly so, finished product. Good apple choices include Golden Delicious, Granny Smith, Gravenstein, McIntosh, Newton, Pippin, or Winesap.

SERVING SUGGESTIONS

- *Spice flavors become heightened when incorporated with a fat, such as butter. To that end, generously slather some apple butter onto a hot, buttered Buttermilk Biscuit (page 147). To me, breakfast doesn't get more iconically Southern than that.*
- *I learned one of my favorite ways to use apple butter from a family friend when I was fifteen: Spread 1 to 2 tablespoons over a graham cracker that you have generously covered with Cream Cheese (page 202).*
- *Your morning oatmeal will come alive by stirring in a good dollop of apple butter.*
- *Consider adding apple butter to plain, whole-milk yogurt, along with some toasted pecans, dried cherries, and a bit of bee pollen for a morning, or anytime, snack.*

APPLE BUTTER

· MAKES 4 TO 5 HALF-PINTS ·

5 pounds cooking apples, peeled, cored, and coarsely chopped

2 cups apple cider

2 cups sugar

2 teaspoons ground cinnamon

½ teaspoon ground cloves

½ teaspoon ground nutmeg

½ teaspoon ground ginger

1. Place the apples and the cider in a large stainless-steel pot. Bring to a boil over medium-high heat. Reduce the heat and simmer for 30 minutes. Stir occasionally to prevent sticking. If more liquid is needed, add water in 2 tablespoon increments. Remove from the heat.

2. Either press the cooked apple mixture through a food mill or fine-mesh sieve, transfer to a food processor once slightly cooled, or use an immersion blender and purée the mixture in the pot. If using a food processor or blender, blend just until smooth but not runny.

3. Once puréed, return the mixture to the pot, and add the sugar, cinnamon, cloves, nutmeg, and ginger. Stir to fully combine and bring to a gentle boil over medium heat. Reduce the heat to low and simmer for 25 to 30 minutes, until the apple butter thickens and clings to the back of a spoon. Stir often to prevent the mixture from sticking. Remove the pot from the heat.

4. While the apple butter cooks, fill a canner or large stockpot with water, place four or five half-pint jars inside, and set over medium-high heat. Bring just to the boiling point.

5. Using a jar lifter, remove the hot jars from the canner and place on top of a kitchen cloth on the counter. With the help of a canning funnel, pack the apple butter into the jars, reserving ¼ inch headspace.

6. Use a spatula or wooden chopstick to remove any trapped air bubbles around the interior circumference of the jars. Wipe the rims clean with a damp cloth. Place on the lids and screw bands, tightening only until fingertip-tight.

7. Again using a jar lifter, slowly place the filled jars in the canner. Be sure that the jars are covered by at least 1 inch of water. Bring to a boil, and then process for 10 minutes, starting the timer once the water is at a full, rolling boil. Adjust for altitude as needed (see page 9 for detailed canning instructions).

BRUSSELS SPROUTS SALAD WITH APPLE BUTTER VINAIGRETTE

· SERVES 4 TO 6 ·

Raw Brussels sprout leaves might not sound delectable, but once they're enrobed in a sweet, spicy apple butter vinaigrette, they become downright transcendent. I know it sounds hyperbolic, but try it before you knock it. As soon as you do, I have no doubt the dish will begin making regular appearances on your dining table when fresh Brussels sprouts are in season.

FOR THE VINAIGRETTE
¼ cup Apple Butter
2 tablespoons Apple Cider Vinegar (page 88)
¼ cup extra-virgin olive oil
½ teaspoon sea salt
Freshly ground black pepper

FOR THE BRUSSELS SPROUTS
4 slices Bacon (page 176)
1 pound Brussels sprouts

1. Preheat the oven to 400°F.
2. Combine the apple butter, vinegar, olive oil, salt, and pepper to taste in a lidded jar. Shake until fully emulsified. Set aside.
3. Place a metal cooling rack over a large rimmed baking sheet. Arrange the bacon slices on the cooling rack and bake for 15 minutes, until browned and fragrant. Once cool to the touch, crumble into small pieces.
4. While the bacon cooks, tear the leaves off each Brussels sprout, leaving behind the innermost core and bottom (discard or compost those pieces).
5. Place the Brussels sprout leaves in a large bowl. Scatter the bacon over the leaves and pour in the vinaigrette. Toss the salad with tongs or a spoon until evenly coated. Serve immediately.

PORK CHOP STACK WITH APPLE BUTTER & CHEDDAR

· SERVES 4 ·

Pork chops are among my favorite ways to dine on swine. Salty, tender, and unctuous, they hit all the right notes without ever seeming to overdo it. Partnered here in layers with apple butter and cheddar, this dish comes together easily and deliciously for a busy weeknight meal.

4 thick-cut boneless pork chops
Sea salt and freshly ground black pepper
2 tablespoons peanut oil
Butter for the baking sheet

4 ounces cheddar cheese, sliced thinly
  or grated
½ cup Apple Butter

1. Sprinkle a bit of salt and pepper on both sides of each pork chop. Place the chops on a large plate or platter and leave them to sit at room temperature for 15 minutes.

2. Warm a medium cast iron skillet over medium-high heat. Add the peanut oil and pork chops, and sear for about 4 minutes on each side. Transfer the pork chops to a plate and let sit for 10 minutes.

3. Preheat the oven to 420°F. On a cutting board, cut each pork chop in half lengthwise to make them half their original thickness. Remove any visible excess fat on the outside.

4. Liberally butter a large rimmed baking sheet and lay the pork chops cut-side down. Top each with about ½ ounce of cheddar cheese.

5. Bake for about 5 to 7 minutes, until the cheese is melted and each chop is cooked through. Remove the chops to a cutting board and let them sit for a couple minutes before plating.

6. To serve, place one pork chop half, cheese-side up, on each plate. Top each with 1 tablespoon of apple butter. Top with the other half of the chop, then another tablespoon of apple butter, creating a stack. Serve immediately.

TOMATO JAM

I am, by nature, not a fan of summer. Though my birthday falls during its tenure, and while I agree that trips to the beach, abundant watermelon consumption, and s'mores rank among its high points, summer and I simply don't get along. My crankiness peaks when the heat and humidity threaten to smother, the mosquitos are in charge, and the yellow jackets are on patrol. What makes June to August bearable to me, though, are tomatoes. Plucked while still warm and heavy with juice, sliced thick, and sandwiched between bread liberally slathered with mayonnaise, tomatoes are my saving grace when the mercury soars.

From my kitchen garden to the countless fields of commercially grown varieties, tomatoes thrive in the Southern states. Originally from Central and South America, it is believed that Spanish colonists brought tomatoes to the Caribbean, and those Caribbean crops eventually made their way to the New World. They are now grown commercially across the southern United States, as well as in California, New Jersey, and Michigan.

Technically a fruit though largely treated as a vegetable, tomatoes are inherently sweet while also possessing a mild sourness. Thus, drawing out and playing upon these flavor profiles in the form of a sweet and sour jam makes sense. This condiment is highly versatile, as welcome on cheeseburgers as it is on scrambled eggs (trust me on that one).

SERVING SUGGESTIONS

- *Tomatoes and cheese pairings share a long history, as the cheese balances out the tartness of the tomatoes. Think pizza, spaghetti with Parmesan, grilled cheese and tomato soup. In that vein, spread some tomato jam on sourdough bread slices, put smoked Gouda or cheddar in between, and grill or press for a grilled cheese sandwich.*
- *Baste onto grilled chicken thighs and legs.*
- *Include on a cheese plate, alongside Bourbon Bacon Jam (page 178), toasted walnuts, Candied Black Walnuts (page 164), Dried Apples (page 133), and a medley of cheeses.*

TOMATO JAM

· MAKES ABOUT 4 HALF-PINTS ·

4 pounds Roma tomatoes, skins on, cored and coarsely chopped

1 cup granulated sugar

½ cup packed light brown sugar

⅓ cup lime juice

1 tablespoon sea salt

2 teaspoons ground allspice

1 teaspoon ground cinnamon

½ teaspoon ground cloves

¼ teaspoon ground cayenne

1. Place the tomatoes, granulated sugar, brown sugar, lime juice, salt, allspice, cinnamon, cloves, and cayenne in a medium stainless-steel pot. Bring to a boil over medium heat, stirring often.

2. Reduce the heat and simmer, stirring occasionally, until the mixture thickens and firms to a jam-like consistency, around 60 to 75 minutes.

3. During the last 20 minutes of cooking time, fill a canner or large stockpot with water, place four or five half-pint jars inside, and set over medium-high heat. Bring just to the boiling point.

4. Using a jar lifter, remove the hot jars from the canner and place on top of a kitchen cloth on the counter. With the help of a canning funnel, pack the tomato jam into the jars, reserving ½ inch headspace.

5. Use a spatula or wooden chopstick to remove any trapped air bubbles around the interior circumference of the jars. Wipe the rims clean with a damp cloth. Place on the lids and screw bands, tightening only until fingertip-tight.

6. Again using a jar lifter, slowly place the filled jars in the canner. Be sure that the jars are covered by at least 1 inch of water. Bring to a boil, and then process for 10 minutes, starting the timer once the water is at a full, rolling boil. Adjust for altitude as needed (see page 9 for detailed canning instructions).

GOAT CHEESE & SMOKED TROUT TOMATO JAM SANDWICHES

· SERVES 4 ·

I find these sandwiches to be absolutely perfect springtime snacks. When asparagus is fresh and appearing at local farmers' markets, grab some and partner it with sturdy bread, creamy goat cheese, smoky trout, and piquant tomato jam for a seasonally delightful sandwich.

---

4 ounces smoked trout or salmon

8 ounces Cream Cheese (page 202)

3 tablespoons extra-virgin olive oil

1 bunch asparagus spears, cut into bite-size pieces

Sea salt and freshly ground black pepper

1 bunch watercress, stalks removed and chopped

¼ lemon

Tomato Jam

Loaf of bread, cut into small rectangles

1. In a food processor, blend the trout and cream cheese until fully combined. Set aside.

2. Heat a cast iron skillet over medium-high heat. Add 1 tablespoon of the olive oil. Sauté the asparagus bites in the oil, until they start to brown, about 6 to 7 minutes, then toss with a pinch of sea salt and a couple grinds of pepper. Remove the pan from the heat.

3. Toss the watercress with the remaining 2 tablespoons olive oil, a squeeze of lemon, and a pinch of sea salt in a medium mixing bowl.

4. Spread the cream cheese mixture over half of the pieces of bread. Spoon about 1 tablespoon of tomato jam onto each piece of bread. Top with asparagus pieces and watercress, and then place the remaining bread on top. Serve immediately.

SOUTHERN TARTINES WITH ROASTED BRUSSELS SPROUTS

· SERVES 3 ·

Essentially the French word for open-faced sandwiches, tartines are gloriously, endlessly customizable. Here is a tartine with a Southern twist: pimento cheese, tomato jam, roasted Brussels sprouts, hard-boiled eggs, and light toppings.

FOR THE BRUSSELS SPROUTS

1 pound Brussels sprouts, stems removed and sprouts halved

3 tablespoons extra-virgin olive oil

¼ teaspoon sea salt

Freshly ground black pepper

FOR THE TARTINES

6 slices toast

¾ cup (12 tablespoons) Pimento Cheese (page 33)

6 tablespoons Tomato Jam

3 hard-boiled eggs, thinly sliced

¼ cup radish slices

6 teaspoons capers

6 teaspoons finely chopped green olives

Chopped parsley

1. Preheat the oven to 450°F.
2. Place the Brussels sprouts, olive oil, salt, and pepper to taste on a large rimmed baking sheet. Using clean hands, toss the ingredients until the sprouts are coated evenly with oil.
3. Roast in the oven for 20 minutes, until the sprouts are crispy and browned. Remove the pan from the oven, and add more salt if desired.
4. Spread 2 tablespoons of pimento cheese on each slice of toast. Top with 1 tablespoon of tomato jam.
5. Evenly divide the hard-boiled egg slices among the pieces of toast. Repeat with the Brussels sprouts, and then the radish slices.
6. Scatter 1 teaspoon of capers and 1 teaspoon of chopped olives over each piece of toast. Finish by scattering chopped parsley evenly across the tartines. Serve immediately.

MUSCADINE JELLY

———

Muscadine and scuppernong grapes grow in abundance throughout the Southern Appalachians. In fact, they can be found growing wild, and are referred to as "fox grapes" all across the Eastern Seaboard. Thick-skinned, large, and riddled with seeds, these grapes belong to one of the two species native to North America. Bronze in color, scuppernongs were the first cultivars of muscadine grapes. They were named after the location of their discovery, along the Scuppernong River in eastern North Carolina.

As a lifelong Southerner, I associate the flavors of muscadines and scuppernongs with the word "grape." Their arrival at farmers' markets serves as the harbinger that autumn is imminent and summer is waning. The flavor of these grapes, best described as heavily floral and musty or "musky," likely accounts for the grape's name.

For optimal success making muscadine jelly, use grapes that you just picked, or that just arrived at the farmers' market. At that time, their inherent pectin is high and they haven't yet become overly ripe, making them more amenable to solidifying into jam once jarred. I found this advice in *The Taste of Country Cooking*, written by acclaimed Southern foods author and historian Edna Lewis.

Muscadine jelly is fabulous slathered liberally across toast and malleable enough to marry well with meats. A lovely hostess or housewarming gift, this jelly really showcases the flavor of the South. Put up some jars when you see these grapes, as their availability is fleeting.

SERVING SUGGESTIONS

- *The heady, ambrosial aroma and flavor of muscadine jelly shines best when not overshadowed by more imposing flavors. Accordingly, spoon a bit over Vanilla Ice Cream (page 210) for a late summer or early autumn treat, and serve with optional slices of Pound Cake (page 229).*
- *Employ as a key ingredient in PB&Js (Peanut Butter, page 78).*
- *Spoon about ½ cup atop a large Brie round, wrap in butter-brushed sheets of phyllo pastry, and bake at 400°F for 15 to 20 minutes, until the pastry turns golden. Serve with crackers.*
- *Use as a filling for thumbprint cookies.*

MUSCADINE JELLY

· MAKES 3 HALF-PINTS ·

2½ pounds muscadine grapes

⅔ cup water

2 cups sugar

1 tablespoon dry pectin

1. Place the grapes and water in a large stainless-steel pot. Using a potato masher or meat tenderizer (or another kitchen tool with a flat side), mash the grapes until a number of them pop and their flesh is exposed.

2. Place over high heat and bring to a boil. Reduce the heat to low and simmer for 15 minutes.

3. Transfer the grape mixture to a jelly bag suspended over a bowl. (A jelly bag is a fine mesh bag placed in a metal frame; you can find them at canning and preserving retailers or online.) Strain the mixture for 8 to 12 hours. Discard or compost the solids.

4. Fill a canner or large stockpot with water and place three half-pint jars inside. Set over high heat and bring just to the boiling point.

5. In a small bowl, mix ¼ cup of the sugar with the pectin. Place the strained liquid and the sugar mixture in a medium pot. Bring to a boil, stir to combine, and then stir in the remaining 1¾ cups sugar. Return the mixture to a boil, stirring to fully combine. Boil hard for 2 minutes, skimming off any foam that forms.

6. Using a jar lifter, remove the hot jars from the canner and place on top of a kitchen cloth on the counter. With the help of a canning funnel, pour the jelly into the jars, reserving ¼ inch headspace.

7. Use a spatula or wooden chopstick to remove any trapped air bubbles around the interior circumference of the jars. Wipe the rims clean with a damp cloth. Place on the lids and screw bands, tightening only until fingertip-tight.

8. Again using a jar lifter, slowly place the filled jars in the canner. Be sure that the jars are covered by at least 1 inch of water. Bring to a boil, and then process for 10 minutes, starting the timer once the water is at a full, rolling boil. Adjust for altitude as needed (see page 9 for detailed canning instructions).

RIBEYE STEAKS WITH MUSCADINE GASTRIQUE

· SERVES 4 ·

A gastrique is made from caramelized sugar deglazed with vinegar, creating a sauce. In this recipe, I use muscadine jelly in lieu of sugar, resulting in a gastrique with ambrosial undertones. Steak offers the perfect foil for this sweet yet sour sauce.

4 ribeye steaks	1 cup Muscadine Jelly
Sea salt	1 cup Apple Cider Vinegar (page 88)
2 tablespoons light olive oil or peanut oil	1 cup red wine, beef broth, or water

1. Preheat the oven to 350°F. Liberally sprinkle the steaks with salt and set aside at room temperature on a large plate or platter for 15 minutes.

2. Warm a cast iron skillet over medium-high heat. Add the oil to the pan. Sear the steaks for about 3 to 4 minutes on each side, turning several times to ensure even cooking.

3. Transfer the pan to the hot oven. Cook for about 5 to 10 minutes, until the steaks reach your desired doneness. Remove the pan from the oven, transfer the steaks to a platter, and allow them to rest about 10 minutes before serving.

4. While the steaks rest, make the gastrique. Warm the same pan you cooked the steaks in over medium-low heat. (Add a light coating of oil, about 1 teaspoon, if the pan is dry.)

5. Add the jelly to the pan and stir for about 1 minute, until it turns syrupy. Add the vinegar and wine, scraping a spatula against the bottom of the pan to deglaze it.

6. Cook the gastrique for about 10 minutes, until it nicely coats the back of a spoon with a syrupy consistency.
7. Plate the steaks individually and top generously with the gastrique. Serve immediately.

PORK MEATBALLS WITH MUSCADINE GLAZE

· SERVES 6 TO 8 ·

When my husband, Glenn, and I were creating recipes for this book, these meatballs disappeared almost as soon as they were done. They're that good. While they'd make a lovely dinner, they'd work equally well served as appetizers at a holiday party or during the big game.

---

3 pieces of rye toast

4 tablespoons extra-virgin olive oil

1 medium onion, diced

3 garlic cloves, minced

3 eggs

½ cup whole milk

2 teaspoons smoked or plain sea salt

2 pounds ground pork

2 teaspoons cumin seeds

Freshly ground black pepper

½ to ¾ cup Muscadine Jelly, depending on desired sweetness

¼ cup crushed peanuts (optional)

1. Put the toast in the food processor. Pulse until fine crumbs form and set aside.
2. Warm 2 tablespoons of the olive oil in a large saucepan over medium-high heat. Add the onion and sauté for 5 minutes. Add the garlic, and stir constantly for 1 minute, then remove the pan from the heat.
3. Whisk the eggs, milk, and salt in a large mixing bowl until fully combined. Add the onion mixture, pork, breadcrumbs, cumin seeds, and several grinds of pepper. Using clean hands, knead all the ingredients together until uniform throughout. Let rest for about 5 minutes, and then shape into meatballs the size of golf balls.
4. Preheat the oven to 350°F.
5. Heat the remaining 2 tablespoons olive oil in the same saucepan over medium-high heat. Cook the meatballs in batches, until browned on all sides, about 6 to 8 minutes.
6. Put the muscadine jelly in a small pot over low heat and stir until warmed throughout and slightly syrupy.
7. Place the meatballs on a large rimmed baking sheet. Pour the warmed jelly over them and gently toss with a spatula until evenly coated. Sprinkle the peanuts, if using, over the meatballs.
8. Bake for 20 minutes, until fragrant and cooked through. Cool for at least 10 minutes before serving.

PEACH CHUTNEY

Chutney might not initially sound like a Southern food. However, when you consider the rich history of cultures, and their foods, that made their way across the seaports of the South, it becomes more logical. Trade outposts from Savannah, Georgia, to Norfolk, Virginia, saw all manner of spices grown in far-flung locales (cloves, cinnamon, mustard seeds, ginger, and nutmeg) brought to the New World and incorporated into Southern kitchens and beyond. An integral component of Indian cuisine, chutneys were introduced to the British during their colonization of India. They were later brought to the British mainland, and eventually made their way to the New World with British colonists.

Chutneys, alongside pickles, jams, jellies, and other preserves, are an excellent way to extend the life of fresh produce, not to mention use a glut of fruit. A combination of vinegar, fruits, spices, and a bit of sugar produces this highly versatile condiment. I've long loved mango chutney, but found that peaches make a more sustainable choice, given that they grow across the South in abundance. When peaches are in season, fill your pantry with this chutney. Delightful on a cold ham sandwich in summer, peach chutney is equally lovely when Jack Frost makes his debut.

SERVING SUGGESTIONS

- *A wide variety of chutneys are integral components of Indian cooking. Playing with those flavors, spread some peach chutney across hot, buttered naan and serve with chicken korma and saag paneer.*
- *Use in a grilled ham and Pimento Cheese (page 33) sandwich or serve alongside roasted chicken and hot rice.*
- *Prepare some over easy eggs and serve on top of soft lettuces like Boston or Bibb with the chutney.*

PEACH CHUTNEY

· MAKES 4 PINTS ·

---

3 pounds peaches, peeled, pitted, and chopped

1 large sweet onion, chopped

¼ cup fresh cherries, pitted and chopped, or ½ cup dried cherries

1 cup dark raisins

½ cup golden raisins

4 garlic cloves, minced

1 tablespoon grated fresh ginger

2 cups light packed brown sugar

3½ cups apple cider vinegar

1 tablespoon mustard seeds

1½ teaspoons red pepper flakes

1 teaspoon ground cinnamon

1. Put the peaches, onion, cherries, both types of raisins, garlic, ginger, sugar, vinegar, mustard seeds, pepper flakes, and cinnamon in a large stainless-steel pot. Bring to a boil over medium-high heat, stirring continuously until the sugar is dissolved, about 6 to 8 minutes.
2. Reduce the heat to low and simmer uncovered for 45 minutes, stirring frequently to keep the chutney from sticking to the pan. If additional liquid is necessary, add water in ¼ cup increments.

3. Fill a canner or large stockpot with water, place four pint jars inside, and set over medium-high heat. Bring just to the boiling point.

4. Using a jar lifter, remove the hot jars from the canner and place on top of a kitchen cloth on the counter. With the help of a canning funnel, pack the chutney into the jars, reserving ½ inch headspace.

5. Use a spatula or wooden chopstick to remove any trapped air bubbles around the interior circumference of the jars. Wipe the rims clean with a damp cloth. Place on the lids and screw bands, tightening only until fingertip-tight.

6. Again using a jar lifter, slowly place the filled jars in the canner. Be sure that the jars are covered by at least 1 inch of water. Bring to a boil, and then process for 10 minutes, starting the timer once the water is at a full, rolling boil. Adjust for altitude as needed (see page 9 for detailed canning instructions).

CURRIED PORK CHOP SANDWICH
WITH PEACH CHUTNEY
· SERVES 4 ·

Mercy, this sandwich is good! It comes together rather quickly and would be most welcome on an autumn picnic or tailgating outside the stadium. It's especially lovely with a hard pear cider or a "Cack-A-Lacky" Ginger Pale Ale produced by Fullsteam Brewery in Durham, North Carolina.

FOR THE COLESLAW

1 medium green cabbage, shredded

2 medium carrots, peeled and shredded

½ cup sea salt or kosher salt

½ cup sugar

½ cup mayonnaise

½ cup Sweet Pickle Relish (page 30)

2 tablespoons prepared yellow mustard

1 teaspoon celery seeds

Freshly ground black pepper

FOR THE PORK CHOP SANDWICH

4 (½-inch-thick) boneless pork chops

1 tablespoon plus 1 teaspoon curry powder

Sea salt and freshly ground black pepper

2 tablespoons extra-virgin olive oil

¼ cup mayonnaise

4 tablespoons Peach Chutney

4 toasted sandwich buns or rolls

1. **PREPARE THE COLESLAW.** Combine the cabbage and carrots with the salt and sugar in a large bowl, and toss until fully incorporated. Let rest for 10 minutes, then rinse thoroughly in a colander under cold running water.

2. Let the mixture sit for 5 minutes longer. Using clean hands, squeeze the vegetables for about 1 minute to help get rid of excess moisture.

3. Wrap the mixture in a kitchen towel or cloth, and squeeze to remove any remaining moisture. Repeat the process with a new towel until no moisture is present.

4. Transfer the mixture to a large bowl. Stir in the mayonnaise, relish, mustard, celery seeds, and several grinds of pepper.

5. Cover with a lid and place in the refrigerator. Cool for at least 1 hour before serving.

6. **PREPARE THE PORK CHOPS.** In a small bowl, combine 1 tablespoon of curry powder with a pinch of salt and several grinds of pepper. Sprinkle this mixture over both sides of each pork chop and set aside on a large plate.

7. Warm the olive oil in a skillet or medium pan over medium-high heat. Add the pork chops, and cook for 6 to 8 minutes, turning frequently, until cooked through and lightly browned. Transfer the chops to a clean plate and leave them to rest for about 5 minutes.

8. Mix the mayonnaise and 1 teaspoon of curry powder in a small bowl.

9. Spread a schmear of the curry mayo and ½ tablespoon of chutney on both halves of the rolls. Top the bottom side of the rolls with one pork chop each and a generous dollop of coleslaw. Top with the top bun and serve immediately.

PEANUT BUTTER

It defies logic to think that one person could single-handedly account for the popularity of a food item. But in the case of peanuts in the United States, this is precisely what happened. Thanks to the tireless efforts of American botanist and inventor George Washington Carver, the consumption and use of peanuts spread across the Southeast, and later, the continental United States.

Over the course of his lifetime, Carver created techniques intended to improve the quality and vitality of subpar soils that had been subjected to repeated plantings of cotton. In an effort to return nitrogen to the soil, he advocated for the use of crop rotation, alternating plantings of sweet potatoes or legumes with cotton plantings. Such crops would imbue the soil with nitrogen, making it healthier, while simultaneously offering crops for human consumption. Carver developed an extension program for training farmers in these crop rotation practices and also provided recipes for preparing and cooking peanuts.

Today, kids and grownups alike agree that peanuts are pretty darn fantastic (except for those with allergies to the legume, of course). Homemade peanut butter is a snap to make, and lacks the fillers, stabilizers, and sweeteners of shelf-ready offerings. I love foods with inspiring stories behind them, and the history of peanuts in the South is as appetizing to learn about as the legumes are to eat.

SERVING SUGGESTIONS

- *Because of its mild flavor, peanut butter can be substituted for other nut or seed butters, such as for tahini in a falafel sauce.*
- *Use to make peanut butter fudge, a Southern classic (truly my Achilles heel!).*
- *Sandwich between some Saltines (page 85) for an instant snack (or a homemade "pack 'o Nabs," as Nanny would have called them).*

PEANUT BUTTER

· MAKES 1½ CUPS ·

2½ cups raw, shelled peanuts
1 tablespoon peanut oil

1 teaspoon sea salt

1. Preheat the oven to 350°F. Spread the peanuts on a large rimmed baking sheet. Roast for 10 minutes, until fragrant and lightly browned. Remove the pan from the oven and set aside to cool for 5 minutes.
2. Transfer the peanuts to a food processor. Process for 1 minute, scrape down the sides of the bowl, and then process for 2 minutes longer. The peanuts will go from looking like dry and gritty granules to clumping into one mass.

3. Scrape down the bowl again. Add the oil and salt, and process for 2 more minutes, until the mixture becomes glossy and smooth.
4. Transfer the peanut butter to a lidded container. Store in the refrigerator and use within 2 to 3 weeks.

FIELD PEA & PEANUT BUTTER HUMMUS

· MAKES 4 CUPS ·

Since peanuts are so strongly associated with the South, it seemed like a natural choice to make a hummus with them instead of tahini. I also subbed field peas for garbanzo beans in this flavorful, close-to-home, protein-rich spread.

1 pound cooked field peas, chilled

1 cup Peanut Butter

½ cup extra-virgin olive oil

Zest and juice of 1 lemon

3 cloves garlic, minced or 1 teaspoon
   granulated garlic

1 teaspoon sea salt

½ teaspoon ground cumin

½ teaspoon ground coriander

Dash of hot sauce

12 ounces cold seltzer

Smoked paprika, olive oil, chopped parsley
   or cilantro, to serve (optional)

1. Put the field peas, peanut butter, olive oil, lemon zest and juice, garlic, salt, cumin, coriander, and hot sauce in a food processor. Process until fully combined.
2. With the machine running, slowly pour in the seltzer water, little by little, until the hummus has a uniformly creamy texture.
3. To serve, top with any or all: a sprinkle of paprika, a drizzle of good olive oil, and a little chopped parsley or cilantro.

SWEET POTATO & PEANUT BUTTER SOUP WITH CRISPY OKRA "CROUTONS"

· SERVES 4 TO 6 ·

Come the first hint of sweater weather, I pretty much want to eat soup and warm sandwiches all day, every day. This soup is perfect for such occasions. Sweet, creamy, with a kiss of spice and a bit of crunch on top, courtesy of the okra "croutons," there's no better soup to spoon when sliding into wool socks for the first time of the season.

FOR THE SOUP

2 pounds sweet potatoes

3 cloves garlic, minced

1 teaspoon coarse sea salt

2 tablespoons extra-virgin olive oil

1 medium onion, diced

1 cup Peanut Butter

4 cups Chicken Stock (page 187)

2 tablespoons Butter (page 194)

1 teaspoon ground cumin

1 teaspoon ground coriander

½ teaspoon ground nutmeg

Chopped cilantro or parsley, to serve
   (optional)

FOR THE OKRA

Peanut oil for frying

½ cup all-purpose flour

Several pinches of sea salt

Freshly ground black pepper

½ pound okra, cut into ½-inch slices

FOR THE PEANUTS

½ cup roasted and salted peanuts

1 teaspoon smoked paprika

1. **PREPARE THE SOUP.** Preheat the oven to 400°F. Place the sweet potatoes on a large rimmed baking sheet, prick several times with a fork, and roast for 1 hour. Remove from the oven and let the potatoes cool for 15 to 20 minutes.

2. Mince the garlic and then chop the salt into it. Leave to rest for about 15 minutes.

3. Warm the olive oil in a medium pot or Dutch oven over medium-high heat. Add the onion and sauté for about 10 minutes, until lightly browned and fragrant.

4. While the onion is cooking, remove the sweet potato flesh (discard or compost the skins). Place the sweet potato flesh, peanut butter, and stock in a food processor (or use an immersion blender) and process until smooth.

5. Add the butter to the onion and stir until it has melted. Add the prepared garlic, and stir for about 1 minute.

6. Add the sweet potato mixture, cumin, coriander, and nutmeg, and stir to fully combine. Cook for about 10 minutes, stirring frequently.

7. Taste, and add salt if desired, keeping in mind that the toppings have a bit of salt.

8. **PREPARE THE OKRA.** Pour ½ inch of peanut oil into a cast iron skillet and warm over medium-high heat.

9. Put the flour, salt, and pepper in a medium mixing bowl. Toss the okra in the flour to fully coat.

10. When the oil is hot, add the okra to the pan. (You'll know the oil is hot enough if the okra sizzles as soon as it's added. If it doesn't sizzle, let the oil heat a bit longer.) Cook for 4 to 5 minutes, turning occasionally, until browned on all sides.

11. Using a slotted spoon or kitchen spider, remove the okra from the pan and place on a plate lined with a paper towel.

12. Prepare the peanuts. In a small bowl, toss the peanuts with the smoked paprika.

13. To serve, ladle the soup into bowls and top with the peanuts, okra, and some chopped cilantro or parsley, if desired.

HOT PEPPER JELLY

Across the Southeast, wherever fried or fatty food is on offer, you'll likely find a jar of hot pepper jelly in the vicinity. A cracker smeared with cream cheese and a dab of pepper jelly is about as classically Southern as a glass of cold sweet tea and a platter of fried chicken. When I was a child, my mom's friends always seemed to have some at the ready for a drop-by visit, or I'd spy a jar on the heavily laden table of a church potluck supper.

Hot pepper jelly is believed to have originated in Lake Jackson, Texas, where it reportedly began being sold commercially in the 1970s. How it spread across the South, I do not know. I can only attest to it now being as common as apple butter and muscadine jelly at farmers' markets and roadside stands.

What I love about the condiment is its versatility. It is truly a pantry staple that proves to be a kitchen workhorse, time and time again. During late summer and early autumn, when gardens and farmers' markets are exploding with sweet and hot peppers, put up some pints of this jelly to inject a bit of heat whenever it's needed.

SERVING SUGGESTIONS

- *The saltiness of strong, sharp cheeses is an excellent contrast to the spicy sweetness of this jelly. To that end, consider using it as a cheese ball ingredient.*
- *Use as a glaze for spatchcocked chicken roasted over a bed of cubed sweet potatoes.*
- *Hot pepper jelly would be a delicious condiment to serve on a cheeseburger.*

HOT PEPPER JELLY

· MAKES 4 HALF-PINTS ·

---

1 red bell pepper, seeded and chopped

2 jalapeño peppers, seeded and chopped

1 poblano pepper, seeded and chopped

1 cup white vinegar

½ cup water

4 cups sugar

One 3-ounce pouch liquid pectin

1. Place the bell, jalapeño, and poblano peppers in a food processor and process until the peppers are in fine-size bits.
2. Transfer the peppers to a small pan, add the vinegar and water, and bring to a boil. Reduce the heat to low and simmer for 10 minutes.
3. Using a fine-mesh sieve, strain off the liquid from the solids. Discard or compost the solids. Pour the liquid into a jelly bag suspended over a bowl. Leave the liquid to strain for 1 hour.
4. About 20 minutes before the end of the straining time, fill a canner or large stockpot with water, place four half-pint jars inside, and set over medium-high heat. Bring just to the boiling point.

5. When the draining time is complete, using the back of a spoon, press the pepper bits in the jelly bag to remove any remaining liquid. Discard or compost the solid pepper bits left in the jelly bag. Place the strained liquid and sugar in a medium pan. Bring to a boil and then stir in the pectin. Return the mixture to a boil, stirring to fully combine. Boil hard for 1 minute, stirring constantly.

6. Using a jar lifter, remove the hot jars from the canner and place on top of a kitchen cloth on the counter. With the help of a canning funnel, pack the pepper jelly into the jars, reserving ¼ inch headspace.

7. Use a spatula or wooden chopstick to remove any trapped air bubbles around the interior circumference of the jars. Wipe the rims clean with a damp cloth. Place on the lids and screw bands, tightening only until fingertip-tight.

8. Again using a jar lifter, slowly place the filled jars in the canner. Be sure that the jars are covered by at least 1 inch of water. Bring to a boil, and then process for 10 minutes, starting the timer once the water is at a full, rolling boil. Adjust for altitude as needed (see page 9 for detailed canning instructions).

HOT PEPPER JELLY CHEESE SPREAD & SALTINES

· MAKES ABOUT 2 CUPS SPREAD AND ABOUT 4 DOZEN CRACKERS ·

A saltine or buttery cracker slathered with cream cheese and garnished with hot pepper jelly is as common a snack in the Southeast as the sight of cotton fields and Piggly Wiggly markets. This combination is ubiquitous for good reason—it's delicious. It makes for a great afternoon pick-me-up or a quick snack to assemble for guests.

FOR THE SALTINES
1½ cups all-purpose flour
3 teaspoons sea salt
½ cup water
2 tablespoons extra-virgin olive oil

FOR THE CHEESE SPREAD
1½ cups Cream Cheese, room temperature (page 202)
1 half-pint (1 cup) Hot Pepper Jelly

1. Preheat the oven to 425°F. Put a rack on the lowest level of the oven. Lightly sprinkle a large rimmed baking sheet with flour.

2. Place the flour and 1 teaspoon of the salt in a medium bowl and whisk until fully combined.

3. Add the water and oil and stir with a metal spoon until all the liquid has been absorbed and the mixture becomes sticky and clumps together.

4. Transfer the dough onto a lightly floured surface. Pat it into a rough square with your hands, and then roll it with a rolling pin as thin as you can without tearing the dough, about ⅛ inch.

5. Using a pastry brush, lightly brush the dough with cold water. Sprinkle the remaining 2 teaspoons salt evenly across the dough's surface.

6. Cut the dough into 1-inch squares with a pointy tip knife, a pizza cutter, or a pie dough cutter.

JAMS & SPREADS

7. Transfer the crackers to the baking sheet. Prick each cracker twice with the tines of a fork.

8. Bake the crackers for 15 to 17 minutes, until their edges have browned slightly. Remove the baking sheet from the oven, cool on the pan for 3 minutes, and then transfer the crackers to a cooling rack. Cool to room temperature before serving. If not serving immediately, transfer the crackers to a lidded airtight container and use within 2 to 3 days.

9. Combine the cream cheese and hot pepper jelly in a medium mixing bowl and stir until fully combined. Serve with the crackers, once they have cooled.

SWEET, SOUR & HOT PORK

· SERVES 8 ·

My grandmother Nanny had a fondness for sweet, fried Chinese foods. Meals out together typically meant dining somewhere with fortune cookies and Chinese zodiac characters printed on the placemats. Without fail, she'd order sweet and sour pork. Considerably less sweet, but equally delicious, here's my take on Nanny's beloved dish.

2 tablespoons extra-virgin olive oil

5 pounds boneless pork shoulder, trimmed of excess fat

1 medium onion, diced

2 bell peppers (any color), diced

3 garlic cloves, minced

⅔ cup Apple Cider Vinegar (page 88)

1 half-pint (1 cup) Hot Pepper Jelly

2 tablespoons Worcestershire sauce

1 cup Ketchup (page 110)

¼ cup soy sauce

1 teaspoon sea salt

Freshly ground black pepper

1 pineapple, peeled, cored, and cubed

Hot Pepper Vinegar, to serve (page 125)

Rice, to serve (optional)

1. Heat the olive oil in a large Dutch oven or heavy pan over medium-high heat. Add the pork and brown on all sides, about 10 minutes. Transfer the pork to a large plate or platter, leaving several tablespoons of oil in the pan.

2. Add the onion and bell peppers to the pan. Sauté for 10 minutes, until they start to brown a little around the edges. Add the garlic and sauté for a couple more minutes.

3. Mix the vinegar, jelly, Worcestershire sauce, ketchup, soy sauce, salt, and several grinds of pepper in a medium bowl. Add the mixture to the pan and simmer for 5 minutes. Add the pork, tossing to coat it evenly in the sauce.

4. Transfer to a slow cooker and cook on low for 8 hours.

5. Remove the pork to a cutting board and set it aside to cool slightly.

6. Transfer the remaining liquid and vegetables to a medium saucepan. Warm over medium heat and reduce by about half, until it is a thick sauce like a gravy.

7. Pull the pork into pieces with a fork, and then toss it with the sauce and the pineapple.

8. Serve over rice, if desired, with hot pepper vinegar on the side.

SAUCES
— & —
VINEGARS

APPLE CIDER VINEGAR

Though apples originated in central Asia, I'd bet that most U.S. residents would claim them as the most iconic American fruit. To get to "as American as apple pie," you've got to start with the ingredients, right? The widespread abundance of apple varieties across the United States, as well as my specific stomping grounds, the Southern Appalachians, has resulted in countless iterations for their use, from Apple Butter (page 62) and Applesauce (page 102) to Mom's Fried Apples (page 196) and so much more.

I find the flavor of apple cider vinegar far superior to white vinegar, as well as considerably smoother and mellower, and just a wee bit sweet. Given all of the apple trees grown here by colonists, it stands to reason that apple cider would be the most commonly employed vinegar across the South.

In my own kitchen, I use apple cider vinegar on a near-daily basis. Whether splashed into a dish for a bit of acid or sipped in small amounts for staving away illness, apple cider vinegar and I have a serious bond. Making a homemade version couldn't be easier. Once you've done the chopping and coring, it's just a matter of waiting, watching, and tasting.

SERVING SUGGESTIONS

- *Add a tablespoon to a hearty lentil soup for a kick of acid to brighten the soup's flavor. Top with Sour Cream (page 207) for extra tang and creaminess.*
- *Use as a key component in making vinaigrettes.*
- *East Carolina–style coleslaw, which is oil and vinegar based, would be an excellent means of employing apple cider vinegar.*

APPLE CIDER VINEGAR

· MAKES 6 TO 8 CUPS ·

6 cups water

½ cup sugar

8 whole organic apples, chopped (leave the peels on and the cores and seeds in, and use a variety of apples)

1. Combine the water and sugar in a medium bowl. Stir until the sugar has fully dissolved.
2. Place the apples in a large nonreactive pot, ceramic pot, or glass bowl. Pour the sugar water over them. The apples need to be fully covered; if they're not, make another batch of sugar water and add just until the apples are covered.
3. Use a large rubber band to secure a triple layer of butter muslin or fine-weave cheesecloth over the top of the pot or bowl. Place in a dark, warm location (such as a pantry, cupboard, top of the refrigerator, or out-of-the-way countertop) for 1 week. If a white, cloudy film forms during the fermenting time, that's fine. If gray, white, green, or other-colored mold or scum forms, your ferment is likely contaminated and it's best to compost this batch and begin anew.

4. After a week, strain the mash from the liquid using a fine-mesh sieve placed atop a bowl. Leave the mixture to strain, covered with a cloth, for at least 8 to 12 hours. Discard or compost the apple pieces.

5. Return the liquid to the container used for fermentation. Replace the cheesecloth or butter muslin, making sure to secure it tightly, and return to the previously used fermenting location.

6. Leave the vinegar to ferment for 3 weeks. Begin tasting it then. If it still tastes fruity and not vinegary, leave it for another week. Once the flavor is to your liking, strain it again through a fine-mesh sieve. Store the vinegar in a lidded container at room temperature. It will keep indefinitely.

NOTE: Homemade apple cider vinegar is not safe to use in home canning. The acidity level of vinegar must be 5% or greater to be considered safe in home canning, otherwise it is not properly acidified and botulism spores can grow, rendering the food unsafe for consumption. Homemade apple cider vinegar levels are highly variable, whereas store-bought offerings are consistently at 5% or greater. Use this vinegar in dishes around the kitchen, but not for long-term preservation. Alternatively, if you'd like, you can purchase pH strips and test the level of each batch of homemade vinegar you make to see if its level is 5% or greater.

BLACK BUTTER GREENS VINEGAR

· MAKES ABOUT 1 CUP ·

Not only does vinegar help bring out the flavor of greens, it activates the release of their calcium and magnesium, making them more bioavailable, a great thing for women. Here, I've added black butter to the vinegar for a depth of flavor. (Note that the butter should be dark brown, not black, when completed; it is called "black butter" from the French *beurre noir*.)

1 cup Apple Cider Vinegar

2 tablespoons brown sugar

2 tablespoons salted butter

1 teaspoon sea salt

Freshly ground black pepper

1 to 2 teaspoons red pepper flakes

Southern Greens (page 20), to serve

1. Warm the apple cider vinegar and brown sugar in a small saucepan over low heat, stirring to combine. Remove from the heat once the sugar dissolves, just before the mixture begins to boil.

2. Melt the butter in a separate saucepan until the solid bits that form at the bottom of the pan are dark brown. Remove the saucepan from the heat.

3. Pour the melted butter into the vinegar mixture. Whisk in the salt, several grinds of pepper, and pepper flakes to taste.

4. Transfer the mixture to a heatproof glass container, such as a Mason jar. Cool to room temperature before using. Serve with Southern Greens. Store in the refrigerator and use within 1 week, warming gently before use.

ROSEMARY APPLE SHRUB

· MAKES ABOUT 3 CUPS ·

A shrub is a vinegar- and fruit-based beverage. Water, either still or sparkling, is added to render it into a thirst-quenching drink. This shrub would be lovely during autumn or early winter, when fresh apple cider is available.

1 cup apple juice or fresh apple cider

¾ cup sugar

1 cup Apple Cider Vinegar

4 large sprigs fresh rosemary

Seltzer or still water

Bourbon (optional)

1. Place the apple juice, sugar, vinegar, and rosemary in a medium pot. Heat over medium-high heat, stirring frequently, until the sugar dissolves but before the mixture begins to boil.
2. Remove the pot from the heat, cover with a lid, and set aside until it cools to room temperature.
3. Strain off the rosemary sprigs and place the shrub in a lidded glass container, such as a Mason jar.
4. To serve, pour about ¼ cup of the shrub into a tall glass, fill with ice, and top off with seltzer or still water (if using bourbon, add about 1 ounce to the glass before filling with the water). Stir and serve immediately. Store any unused portion in the refrigerator and use within 1 month.

BARBEQUE SAUCE

No Southern kitchen is fully equipped without a reliable, go-to barbeque recipe. Its uses are countless. Feel free to double or triple the recipe if your household tends to consume a lot of barbeque sauce. Though this sauce is my husband, Glenn's, own creation, it could be considered a Western North Carolina–style sauce, which is similar to a Kansas City–style sauce. The tomato-less, vinegar-based sauces of Eastern North Carolina, which I grew up on, are great when you want to let the subtleties of the meat shine through, but the bold, contrasting flavors of this sauce are perfect for those times when you are craving a flavor extravaganza.

Glenn developed this recipe over time, adjusting and altering it extensively over the years. I love this quote from him about the recipe: "Sometimes I am in the mood to hear an expert fiddler on their own, or maybe with a couple other instruments to back them up, but there are other times when I'm in the mood for a symphony, or even a marching band. When you are feeling the latter, this is your sauce."

According to food historian Ken Albala, barbeque sauce is "very medieval," because it is full of contrasting flavors, such as sweet, sour, and umami. Later, European cuisines moved more to flavor pairing, rather than balancing flavor contrasts. This style of sauce, with its balanced array of bold flavors, harkens back to the complex flavors of medieval times, as well as the deep, complex flavors of Indian cuisine.

Sorghum gives this sauce a unique, earthy flavor, but maple syrup is a perfectly fine substitute. In fact, substitute any ingredient that you want! Barbeque sauce should be a balance of complex flavors, but there are no rules as to how you arrive there. Puréed mushrooms are every bit as fine of a base as ketchup. If you are in New Mexico, you might want to mix in some Hatch chiles, or if you are in Oregon, some marionberry purée might make it shine. Whatever you do, give it a taste, and adjust the flavorings to your preferences if necessary. As Glenn says, "Good barbeque sauce is full of playfulness and soul."

SERVING SUGGESTIONS

- *This sauce would be a fantastic marinade base for grilled shrimp, as it would tenderize and simultaneously impart flavor.*
- *Mix with a bit of mayonnaise to create a well-balanced aioli.*
- *Drizzle over twice-baked potatoes and serve alongside some grilled broccoli rabe.*
- *Kids love the sweetness of this sauce. Use it as a dip for chicken tenders.*

BARBEQUE SAUCE

· MAKES 2 TO 3 HALF-PINTS ·

1½ cups Ketchup (page 110)

½ cup sorghum syrup

1 tablespoon Worcestershire sauce

1 tablespoon prepared brown mustard

1 tablespoon granulated garlic

2 teaspoons smoked paprika

1 teaspoon ground allspice

1 teaspoon smoked or plain sea salt

Dash of hot sauce

1. Whisk the ketchup, sorghum syrup, Worcestershire sauce, mustard, garlic, paprika, allspice, salt, and hot sauce in a medium bowl until fully combined.

2. Store in the refrigerator and use within 2 weeks. Alternatively, you can preserve the sauce by water bath canning. If you go that route, I suggest doubling the recipe to make it worth your time. Begin by warming the mixture in a small pot on the stove just to the boiling point.

3. While the mixture warms, fill a canner or large stockpot with water, place two or three half-pint jars (or 5 if you have doubled the recipe) inside, and set over medium-high heat. Bring just to the boiling point.

4. Using a jar lifter, remove the hot jars from the canner and place on top of a kitchen cloth on the counter. With the help of a canning funnel, pack the barbeque sauce into the jars, reserving ½ inch headspace.

5. Use a spatula or wooden chopstick to remove any trapped air bubbles around the interior circumference of the jars. Wipe the rims clean with a damp cloth. Place on the lids and screw bands, tightening only until fingertip-tight.

6. Again using a jar lifter, slowly place the filled jars in the canner. Be sure that the jars are covered by at least 1 inch of water. Bring to a boil, and then process for 10 minutes, starting the timer once the water is at a full, rolling boil. Adjust for altitude as needed (see page 9 for detailed canning instructions).

PULLED PORK & BARBEQUE SAUCE

· SERVES 8 TO 10 ·

Pulled pork is one of those dishes that it seems everyone can get behind. Aside from those who fully abstain from meat consumption, I've yet to hear disappointment at the mention of pulled pork for dinner. This recipe lets a slow cooker, that infinitely handy kitchen tool, do most of the work for you.

4 pounds boneless Boston butt

1 tablespoon smoked or plain sea salt

2 tablespoons Bacon Drippings (page 176)

2 large onions, sliced

3 garlic cloves, minced

3 tablespoons light brown sugar

1 cup water

1 cup white wine

½ cup Apple Cider Vinegar (page 88)

3 tablespoons natural liquid smoke

3 tablespoons Worcestershire sauce

2 tablespoons smoked paprika

2 teaspoons ground coriander

Freshly ground black pepper

Barbeque Sauce

1. Remove the pork butt from the refrigerator. Place it on top of a large plate or platter. Sprinkle the salt over it evenly, and leave to rest at room temperature for 15 minutes.

2. Warm the bacon grease in a large pan or Dutch oven over medium-high heat. Add the Boston butt and brown on all sides, turning the meat frequently, for about 10 minutes, until evenly browned. Transfer the meat to a large plate or platter and set aside.

3. Add the onions to the pan and sauté for 8 to 10 minutes, until they start to brown around the edges and become fragrant. Add the garlic and cook for 2 minutes, then add the brown sugar and cook for 2 minutes longer. Add the water, wine, vinegar, liquid smoke, Worcestershire sauce, paprika, coriander, and several grinds of pepper, and cook for 15 minutes. Remove the pan from the heat.

4. Spoon half of the onion mixture into a slow cooker, add the meat, and then spoon the remaining portion of the onion mixture over the meat. Cook for 8 hours on the low setting.

5. Remove the meat from the slow cooker and set aside on a large plate or platter.

6. Pour the onion mixture into a medium saucepan and cook over medium-low heat for 15 to 20 minutes, until the sauce reduces and thickens.

7. Shred the pork with two forks, then toss in a bowl with the onion mixture. Add barbeque sauce to taste and stir until fully combined. Serve immediately.

SLOW COOKER BARBEQUE CHICKEN

· SERVES 4 TO 6 ·

Another means of slow cooking meat, this recipe renders the moistest, tastiest barbequed chicken I have ever had the pleasure of eating. Feel free to adjust the amount of sauce to your liking.

1 whole chicken, about 3½ to 4½ pounds

2 large onions, roughly chopped

1½ cups Barbeque Sauce

2 teaspoons sea salt

Hot sauce, to serve (optional)

1. Remove the skin from the chicken. Set aside the remaining whole chicken on a large plate or platter.

2. Cook the chicken skin over medium heat in a medium saucepan until it gives off a little more than a tablespoon of fat. Remove the skin from the pan and discard it (or give it to your dogs like I do!).

3. Sauté the onions in the chicken fat for about 10 minutes, until they have browned around the edges.

4. Put the onions in the bottom of a slow cooker followed by the chicken, breast side up. Pour 1 cup of the barbeque sauce over the chicken. Cook on low for 6 hours.

5. Pull the chicken out of the pot with tongs, and set aside on a large plate or platter.

6. Pour the onions and juices into a medium saucepan. Add the salt and cook over medium heat until the sauce reduces and thickens, 15 to 20 minutes. Remove the pan from the heat.

7. Pull the chicken off the carcass with a fork, shredding it into medium-size pieces. Stir the pulled chicken, along with the remaining ½ cup barbeque sauce, into the pan of sauce. Taste for salt, and serve with hot sauce on the side, if desired.

FERMENTED HOT SAUCE

Hot sauce is much loved in the South. Head to any restaurant specializing in Southern foods and you'll find a bottle, if not four, on the table. Folks put a drop, or a dousing, on everything from eggs to Shrimp & Grits (page 140) to Sausage Gravy with Buttermilk Biscuits (page 185) and far beyond. Some folks, including my husband, Glenn, and superstar Beyoncé, even carry jars of it in their bag when out and about, so fervent is their devotion.

All hot sauces, however, are far from the same. The peppers used in hot sauces vary widely; some contain fruits, or even unusual vegetables, like sweet potatoes. There's also the production manner to be considered. Sauces that are blended, strained, and then bottled, making them shelf-stable, are quite different from those produced through fermentation.

Shelf-stable hot sauces have been sterilized to kill off, or greatly reduce, bacteria and pathogens. Hot sauces that have undergone fermentation, however, have not been sterilized. Accordingly, "good" or probiotic bacteria are allowed to thrive. As their numbers grow, inherent lactic acid bacteria on the skins of the peppers consume the sugars also naturally present. Once consumed, the sugars are converted to lactic acid, among other things, which ferments the peppers and forms a type of food preservation.

The hot sauce I'm offering here is fermented. Massive thanks to my friend Adriana Oliveira for sharing her recipe, and for the hands-on tutorial she gave me in her home kitchen one balmy August afternoon in 2016. A native of Brazil, Adriana loves all things hot and spicy, as well as fermented, and the hot sauce she created is absolutely delicious.

SERVING SUGGESTIONS

- *Partner with scrambled eggs, Breakfast Sausage (page 182), and avocado slices for a hearty, healthy breakfast that balances heat, creaminess, and herbaceousness.*
- *Stir into and drizzle over beef tacos for some added heat.*
- *Cut cucumbers into thick slices and toss with the hot sauce. Mix in a bit of Sour Cream (page 207) if you need to temper the heat.*
- *Serve as a condiment option with Cornmeal Catfish (page 154).*

FERMENTED HOT SAUCE

· MAKES 2 TO 3 CUPS ·

1 pound hot peppers (a mixture of types is best)

8 medium garlic cloves, peeled

1 apple, cored and cut into slices

1 teaspoon sea salt

1. Put the peppers, garlic, apple, and salt in a food processor or blender. Process until well combined.
2. Open outdoors or with an oven hood on high, as the volatile oils from the hot peppers will be released and they can cause coughing, sneezing, and watery eyes.

3. Using kitchen gloves (you don't want to get any of the pepper sauce on your skin), transfer the mixture to a glass container such as a Mason jar. Cover with a lid, but not too tightly.

4. Leave in a conspicuous location at room temperature for 3 days. Give the jar a gentle shake each day, and remove any visible mold that forms.

5. After 3 days, transfer the hot sauce to the refrigerator. It will keep for about 1 month once refrigerated.

SPICY CHICKEN & VEGETABLE SOUP

· SERVES 6 TO 8 ·

If you crave chicken soup when you feel under the weather, as I frequently do, then this recipe is for you. In addition to nourishing meat, vegetables, and broth, a bit of hot sauce helps clear congestion and keeps your sinuses active and alert.

---

3 tablespoons extra-virgin olive oil

1 large onion, diced

2 carrots, diced

1 red bell pepper, diced

2 stalks celery, diced

8 ounces button or cremini mushrooms, coarsely chopped

8 cups Chicken Stock (page 187)

1 pint (2 cups) Canned Tomatoes (page 120)

2 teaspoons sea salt

Meat from 1 whole cooked chicken, pulled from the bone and roughly chopped

Fermented Hot Sauce

1½ cups frozen or fresh corn

Sour cream, parsley, and cilantro, to serve (optional)

1. Warm the olive oil in a medium saucepan over medium-high heat. Add the onion, carrots, bell pepper, celery, and mushrooms, and sauté for about 20 minutes, until the vegetables are softened and fragrant and beginning to brown around the edges.

2. Add the stock, tomatoes, salt, chicken, and hot sauce to taste (a tablespoon for a little zing, two to make it spicier, three to make it very spicy, etc.). Turn down the heat and gently simmer for 45 minutes.

3. Add the corn and simmer for 10 minutes longer. Taste and adjust for salt and spiciness. Remove the pot from the heat.

4. Ladle the soup into bowls. Serve with a dollop of sour cream and a sprinkle of parsley or cilantro if desired, plus more hot sauce on the side for the adventurous.

HOT CORN RELISH

· SERVES 6 TO 8 ·

This relish is deeply versatile, working as well as a side dish as it would as a topping for tacos, grilled fish, or quesadillas. The hot sauce is truly hot, so if the amount called for feels too intense for you, by all means don't hesitate to scale it back.

2 tablespoons extra-virgin olive oil

1 medium onion, diced

1 red bell pepper, diced

1 cup Apple Cider Vinegar (page 88)

¼ cup sugar

3 cups fresh cut corn (or frozen corn brought to room temperature)

2 teaspoons sea salt

¼ cup Fermented Hot Sauce

1. Warm the olive oil in a large pot or Dutch oven over medium heat. Add the onion and bell pepper, and sauté for 10 minutes.

2. Add the vinegar and sugar, and simmer for 5 minutes. Add the corn and simmer for 20 minutes longer, until the liquid no longer pools in the bottom of the pan. Stir in the salt and then remove from the heat.

3. Stir in the hot sauce. Let the relish cool to room temperature and then serve or store in a lidded container in the refrigerator. Consume within 5 to 7 days.

APPLESAUCE

As discussed with Apple Butter (page 62) and Apple Cider Vinegar (page 88), apples and the Southern Appalachian region have a long history. In every state I've lived in or driven through across the region, I have found apples, either fresh from an orchard or from somewhere within the state. Their versatility is no doubt a large part of their appeal, as you can use them for vinegars, beverages, condiments, and more.

While I take a good deal of apples from my mother's apple tree at her home in Burnsville, North Carolina, I also enjoy packing my family into the car and heading to neighboring Hendersonville County. There we climb a steep, winding road, ultimately ending up at Sky Top Orchard in Flat Rock, North Carolina. From August to November, the orchard is crowded with a wide variety of apples and busloads of schoolchildren making pilgrimages to enjoy them.

Never content to simply grab a bag of apples and go, we enjoy all the open-air amenities at Sky Top. From the petting zoo and hayrides to the bamboo forest and the children's playhouses, we make a day of it, gorging ourselves in between activities with a picnic lunch and the orchard's homemade apple cider donuts and fresh cider.

I make this applesauce every year, and lots of it. It's a pantry staple that is so easy that I just can't justify buying it readymade. I keep the skins on my apples, as I prefer the thickness they offer the completed sauce, as well as the nutrition retained in their peels. That said, if peels don't appeal to you, feel free to remove them, especially if your apples aren't organically grown.

SERVING SUGGESTIONS

- *Apples regularly show up in baked goods as their flavors are easy to mix with a wide range of spices and herbs. Consider baking some applesauce into a Bundt cake or cake squares. It can also replace a bit of the fat called for in a recipe.*
- *Spoon over plain yogurt and splash in a wee bit of vanilla extract for a quick, nutritious snack.*
- *Use as a topping for Buttermilk Pancakes (page 201).*
- *Warm, top with cinnamon, and serve with Pound Cake slices (page 229).*

APPLESAUCE

· MAKES 4 PINTS ·

---

6 pounds apples, cored and roughly chopped   1½ cups fresh apple cider

1. Bring the apples and cider to boil in a large pot. Reduce heat to low, cover with a lid, and simmer over medium heat, stirring occasionally, until the apples have softened and broken down, 20 to 25 minutes.
2. Remove the pot from the heat. Take off the lid, and allow the sauce to cool in the pot for 10 to 15 minutes.

3. While the applesauce cools, fill a canner or large stockpot with water, place four pint jars inside, and set over medium-high heat. Bring just to the boiling point.

4. Process the applesauce to your preferred consistency by mashing with a potato masher, processing in the pot with an immersion blender, or transferring to a food processor and puréeing.

5. Using a jar lifter, remove the hot jars from the canner and place on top of a kitchen cloth on the counter. With the help of a canning funnel, pack the applesauce into the jars, reserving ½ inch headspace.

6. Use a spatula or wooden chopstick to remove any trapped air bubbles around the interior circumference of the jars. Wipe the rims clean with a damp cloth. Place on the lids and screw bands, tightening only until fingertip-tight.

7. Again using a jar lifter, slowly place the filled jars in the canner. Be sure that the jars are covered by at least 1 inch of water. Bring to a boil, and then process for 10 minutes, starting the timer once the water is at a full, rolling boil. Adjust for altitude as needed (see page 9 for detailed canning instructions).

HASH BROWN STACK WITH APPLESAUCE

· SERVES 4 ·

A well-known, well-loved breakfast chain in the South offers hash browns "scattered, smothered, covered, and chunked," depending on how you want them topped. This recipe takes that idea as its starting point, incorporating breakfast sausage and applesauce into the mix. The toppings on this dish can be altered however you want, using the hash browns as a base. Less meat and vegetables makes it more of a side dish, while the amount called for makes it more of an entrée.

1½ pounds Yukon gold potatoes	1 red bell pepper, diced
1 teaspoon sea salt	½ pound mushrooms, sliced
1 pound Breakfast Sausage (page 182)	4 ounces cheddar cheese, grated
6 tablespoons extra-virgin olive oil	½ cup Applesauce
1 medium onion, diced	Chopped parsley, to serve (optional)

1. Preheat oven to 350°F. Lightly oil two large rimmed baking sheets. Set aside.

2. Wash and shred the potatoes. Rinse the shredded potatoes in a colander under cold running water for 2 minutes, until the water runs clear.

3. Place the potatoes in a kitchen cloth and squeeze firmly. Change towels and squeeze again.

4. Transfer the potatoes to a medium bowl and toss with the salt. Divide the potatoes between the two baking sheets, spreading them out evenly. Bake for 12 minutes, trading racks halfway through. Remove the baking sheets from the oven.

5. Cook the sausage in a 12-inch cast iron skillet over medium heat for 7 to 8 minutes, until cooked through. Remove the sausage and transfer it to a small bowl.

6. Add 2 tablespoons of the olive oil to the same pan and set over medium-high heat. Add the onion, bell pepper, and mushrooms, and sauté for 20 minutes, until browned around the edges.

Remove the pan from the heat and transfer the vegetables to a small bowl.

7. Pour 1 tablespoon of the remaining olive oil over one of the sheets of baked shredded potatoes. Toss to combine the oil and potatoes.

8. Add 1 tablespoon of the remaining olive oil to the cast iron skillet over medium heat. Put the potatoes that you just oiled into the pan and press down gently to make them evenly thick. Cook until golden brown, 10 to 12 minutes.

9. Using pot holders, invert the hash browns onto a dinner plate. Invert again onto another plate, so that the uncooked side is facing up. Add 1 tablespoon of the remaining olive oil to the pan to lightly coat and then carefully invert the potatoes into the pan, uncooked side down. Cook for 5 minutes, until golden brown, then invert onto a cookie sheet and hold in the warm oven. Repeat the process with the second half of the potatoes and the remaining 1 tablespoon olive oil.

10. Meanwhile, warm the meat with the veggies.

11. On a round platter or large dinner plate, center one of the cooked hash browns. Spread ¼ cup of the applesauce over the hash browns. Layer 2 ounces of the cheese over the applesauce and spread half of the meat and vegetable mixture over the cheese. Place the second portion of hash browns over that. Repeat with the remaining ¼ cup applesauce, 2 ounces cheese, and meat/vegetable mixture. Top with parsley, if using. Serve immediately.

GRIT CAKES WITH COUNTRY HAM & APPLESAUCE

· SERVES 6 ·

This dish is plenty filling for a busy day ahead while also elegant enough to serve at a special occasion brunch or holiday meal. If you're feeding a crowd, simply double the recipe, as each guest should be served two grit cakes apiece.

4 cups cooked Grits (page 138)

4 or 5 tablespoons Butter (page 194)

6 ounces hoop cheese or cheddar cheese, grated

4 ounces country ham

¾ cup Applesauce

Chopped parsley, to serve (optional)

1. Evenly butter a 12-cup muffin tin with 1 tablespoon of the butter and divide the grits evenly between the cups.

2. Place in the refrigerator and chill for 8 to 12 hours.

3. Run a knife around the grit cakes and pop them out.

4. Heat 2 tablespoons of the remaining butter over medium heat in a 10- or 12-inch cast iron skillet. Cook the grit cakes a few at a time, for about 4 minutes on each side. Flip very carefully, adding a little more butter to the pan between turns, if necessary. Top each cake with ½ tablespoon of the cheese after flipping. Continue until you have cooked all the grit cakes. Set aside.

5. In a separate skillet or saucepan, cook the country ham over medium heat in the remaining 1 tablespoon butter, until cooked through, about 5 to 7 minutes.

6. Serve the grit cakes topped with a little country ham, 1 tablespoon applesauce, and a sprinkle of parsley, if using.

CHILE SAUCE

My husband, Glenn, grew up with his mother making this chile sauce, which is based on an old family recipe dating back to the 1800s. Wanting to unearth a bit more of the sauce's family history, I reached out to Suzanne English, my sister-in-law and the family's unofficial genealogist. "My grandmother spelled it chile sauce with an 'e.' I thought perhaps she may have been misspelling it, so I looked at newspapers from 1880–1940 and, sure enough, there were many recipes for chile sauce, similar to hers, spelled with an "e," especially around the turn of the century (1900–1908), and most of these were in Southern papers. The recipe seems to be a common part of the repertoire in a turn of the century housewife's kitchen," Suzanne wrote in reply to my e-mail query.

It turns out the recipe was given to Glenn and Suzanne's grandmother by a woman named Lillian Miles. According to family folklore, Lillian, originally from Kentucky, was sent back east at age five after her mother died with a note pinned to her coat requesting that she be reared by relatives. Lillian would later take on a nanny/caretaker role for Suzanne's grandmother and all her siblings, and as such, became quite dear to Grandma English. This chile sauce of Lillian's has been passed down in the English family through the generations, which is how I ultimately ended up with it.

Suzanne went on to relay the ultimate mission of the sauce. "The idea of chile sauce was to use up the great abundance of tomatoes and peppers grown in the kitchen garden and create them into something that kept through the winter and was used as a condiment. Canning was done by the women at the end of the summer, and I can remember my grandmother, mother, and aunts all working for days canning peaches, tomatoes, and chile sauce. The most delicious and best smelling was the chile sauce, as the spices and fragrance filled the entire house while it cooked for hours on top of the stove. As kids we used to steal the jars from my mother's stash and eat it right out of the jar."

I have found chile sauce to be amenable to all manner of applications. There are few things it doesn't pair well with. Don't be put off by the large volume of vegetables required; they cook down considerably.

SERVING SUGGESTIONS

- *Slow-cooked meats take very well to this sauce. Consider using in a pot roast or in making beef stew, as it both tenderizes and flavors the dish.*
- *Use as an ingredient in homemade Thousand Island dressing.*
- *Stir in as a flavorful addition to Meatloaf with Ketchup Crust (page 113).*
- *Incorporate into a dipping sauce for shrimp cocktail.*

CHILE SAUCE

· MAKES 6 TO 8 HALF-PINTS ·

18 large tomatoes, cored

5 green peppers, seeded

5 large onions, chopped

3 cups apple cider vinegar (see Note)

1½ cups sugar

3 tablespoons sea salt

2 teaspoons ground ginger

2 teaspoons ground cloves

2 teaspoons ground allspice

NOTE: As per the note about the variable acidity of homemade apple cider vinegar on page 90, use store-bought vinegar here (since the jars will be water bath canned), or purchase pH strips and perform an acidity test.

1. Place the tomatoes, peppers, and onions in a food processor or blender. Pulse several times, until the mixture is the consistency of chunky tomato sauce but not uniformly smooth.

2. Transfer the vegetable mixture to a large pot or Dutch oven. Add the vinegar, sugar, salt, ginger, cloves, and allspice. Stir to fully combine.

3. Bring to a gentle boil. Reduce the heat to low and simmer for 3 to 3½ hours, until the sauce has darkened in color, reduced in volume by about half, and clings to the back of a spoon.

4. During the last 20 minutes of cooking time, fill a canner or large stockpot with water, place six to eight half-pint jars inside, and set over medium-high heat. Bring just to the boiling point.

5. Using a jar lifter, remove the hot jars from the canner and place on top of a kitchen cloth on the counter. With the help of a canning funnel, pack the chile sauce into the jars, reserving ½ inch headspace.

6. Use a spatula or wooden chopstick to remove any trapped air bubbles around the interior circumference of the jars. Wipe the rims clean with a damp cloth. Place on the lids and screw bands, tightening only until fingertip-tight.

7. Again using a jar lifter, slowly place the filled jars in the canner. Be sure that the jars are covered by at least 1 inch of water. Bring to a boil, and then process for 10 minutes, starting the timer once the water is at a full, rolling boil. Adjust for altitude as needed (see page 9 for detailed canning instructions).

CHICKEN FRIED SHRIMP WITH COMEBACK SAUCE

· SERVES 4 TO 6 ·

Chicken fried–anything is highly popular in Southern cooking. Here I'm applying that technique to shrimp. The sauce is named for how tasty it is—you'll definitely want to "come back" for more.

FOR THE COMEBACK SAUCE

1 cup mayonnaise

½ cup Chile Sauce

1 tablespoon lemon juice

1 tablespoon Worcestershire sauce

1 tablespoon prepared brown mustard

2 teaspoons prepared horseradish

2 teaspoons granulated garlic

1 teaspoon smoked paprika

Dash of hot sauce (optional)

FOR THE SHRIMP

Peanut oil for frying

1½ pounds large shrimp, peeled and deveined

1 cup Buttermilk (page 199)

1 egg

Dash of hot sauce

2 teaspoons sea salt

1½ cups all-purpose flour

1 teaspoon granulated garlic

1 teaspoon granulated onion

Freshly ground black pepper

1. Whisk the mayonnaise, chile sauce, lemon juice, Worcestershire sauce, mustard, horseradish, garlic, paprika, and hot sauce, if using, in a medium bowl until fully combined. Keep the sauce in the refrigerator until serving time.

2. Pour about ¼ inch of peanut oil into a large cast iron skillet. Set over medium heat and let it heat up for about 10 minutes while preparing the ingredients.

3. In a small mixing bowl, whisk the buttermilk with the egg, hot sauce, and 1 teaspoon of the salt.

4. In a separate bowl, mix the flour with the remaining 1 teaspoon salt, garlic, onion, and several grinds of pepper. Dredge each shrimp in the flour mixture and set them on a large plate or platter.

5. Dunk each shrimp in the buttermilk mixture and then dredge them in the flour again.

6. Using a cooking thermometer, check to see if the heating oil is at least 350°F to 360°F. Once heated to temperature, cook the shrimp in batches, about 2 minutes per side, until golden brown. Remove the shrimp with a kitchen spider and place them on a cooling rack.

7. Once all the shrimp are cooked, serve immediately with the comeback sauce.

CATFISH IN CHILE SAUCE

· SERVES 4 ·

If you find yourself in a too-busy-to-cook scenario, turn to this recipe. It cooks up in a flash and can be on the table in under 30 minutes. Save delivery for another night.

2 tablespoons toasted sesame oil

1½ pounds catfish fillets

1 pint (2 cups) Chile Sauce

3 cups cooked white rice

1. Warm the oil in a medium saucepan over medium heat. Add the catfish and sauté for 2 minutes per side.

2. Add the chile sauce, reduce the heat to low, and simmer for 20 minutes, stirring occasionally, breaking up the fish.

3. Serve over rice with hot sauce on the side.

SAUCES & VINEGARS

KETCHUP

For a condiment as beloved as it is in the United States, ketchup's origins are anything but native. Derived from the Hokkien Chinese word *ke-tsiap*, a sauce created with fermented fish, ketchup had a rather circuitous history from Southeast Asia to the shores of the New World. Apparently, traders brought fish sauce to Southeast China, where British soldiers purportedly first sampled it. Upon returning home, they attempted to recreate it.

Early British iterations of ketchup were nothing like the thick, red sauce we know today. Using ingredients including mushrooms, oysters, or even anchovies, these sauces attempted to reference the umami flavors enjoyed in Asia. More similar in appearance and consistency to Worcestershire sauce, ketchup was far removed from what it has become due to lacking one key ingredient—tomatoes.

Following the introduction of tomatoes to the condiment sometime in the nineteenth century, people began experimenting with different versions of ketchup to render it shelf-stable (capable of withstanding long periods of preservation). Henry J. Heinz of Pittsburgh debuted the version that would go on to epitomize what ketchups should resemble. His product began dominating the market in the early twentieth century, and has continued to do so.

So why bother making your own? As with most things, it comes down to flavor. Homemade ketchup is worth the work. It tastes fresh and bright in a way that its store-bought kin simply cannot, especially if your tomatoes are just or recently picked, at their peak of ripeness. Tomatoes grow abundantly throughout the Southeast, and fresh specimens are never hard to find come high summer. If you go through a good deal of ketchup, you may want to double or triple this recipe to have a pantry's worth all year.

SERVING SUGGESTIONS

- *Serves a key role in Sweet, Sour & Hot Pork (page 83), as it imparts the otherwise neutral flavor profile of pork with tang and zest.*
- *Use as a condiment for Sweet Potato French Fries (page 175).*
- *Be iconoclastic like my cousin Keri and serve with scrambled eggs.*
- *Stir in a bit of Fermented Hot Sauce (page 97) for an instant salsa of sorts.*

KETCHUP

· MAKES 4 HALF-PINTS ·

---

4 pints (8 cups) Canned Tomatoes
  (page 120)

1 medium onion, chopped

1 red bell pepper, chopped and seeded

¾ cup packed light brown sugar

4 cups apple cider vinegar (see Note)

2 teaspoons sea salt

2 bay leaves

1 teaspoon black peppercorns

1 teaspoon whole allspice

1 teaspoon mustard seeds

1 teaspoon celery seeds

½ teaspoon whole cloves

NOTE: As per the note about the variable acidity of homemade apple cider vinegar on page 90, use store-bought vinegar here (since the jars will be water bath canned), or purchase pH strips and perform an acidity test.

1. Purée the tomatoes, onion, and bell pepper in a blender or food processor until smooth.
2. Transfer the mixture to a medium pot and bring to a boil over medium-high heat. Reduce the heat to low, cover with a lid, and simmer for 30 minutes.
3. Stir in the brown sugar, vinegar, and salt. Place the bay leaves, black peppercorns, allspice, mustard seeds, celery seeds, and cloves in a small muslin bag or large tea ball, and add to the pot.
4. Cover the pot and simmer for 1½ hours, stirring frequently, until the sauce has thickened and reduced. Remove the spice bag from the sauce and discard or compost the solids.
5. During the last 20 minutes of cooking time, fill a canner or large stockpot with water, place four half-pint jars inside, and set over medium-high heat. Bring just to the boiling point.
6. Using a jar lifter, remove the hot jars from the canner and place on top of a kitchen cloth on the counter. With the help of a canning funnel, pack the ketchup into the jars, reserving ¼ inch headspace.
7. Use a spatula or wooden chopstick to remove any trapped air bubbles around the interior circumference of the jars. Wipe the rims clean with a damp cloth. Place on the lids and screw bands, tightening only until fingertip-tight.
8. Again using a jar lifter, slowly place the filled jars in the canner. Be sure that the jars are covered by at least 1 inch of water. Bring to a boil, and then process for 10 minutes, starting the timer once the water is at a full, rolling boil. Adjust for altitude as needed (see page 9 for detailed canning instructions).

BLUEBERRY KETCHUP

· MAKES 3 TO 4 HALF-PINTS ·

When I was a child, my grandmother Nanny owned a U-pick blueberry farm in Chesapeake, Virginia. Whenever I have blueberries now (and I do in abundance each year, as we have seventeen bushes planted beside our house), I'm transported to days well spent on her farm, picking berries, getting chased by her goat Howard, sneaking up on bullfrogs in her pond, and digging up potatoes in the garden. Try this ketchup on a burger with some strong cheese, or as a dipping sauce for Sweet Potato French Fries (page 175).

4 cups fresh blueberries
⅔ cup packed light brown sugar
⅔ cup apple cider vinegar (see Note)
3 tablespoons lemon juice

1 teaspoon sea salt
1 teaspoon black pepper
1 cup Ketchup

NOTE: As per the note about the variable acidity of homemade apple cider vinegar on page 90, use store-bought vinegar here (since the jars will be water bath canned), or purchase pH strips and perform an acidity test.

1. Bring the blueberries, brown sugar, vinegar, lemon juice, salt, and pepper to a boil in a medium saucepan, and stir until the brown sugar has fully dissolved.
2. Reduce the heat and simmer for 20 minutes, stirring frequently, until the blueberry mixture has noticeably thickened. Remove the pan from the heat and set aside to cool for 10 minutes.
3. While the sauce simmers, fill a canner or large stockpot with water, place four half-pint jars inside, and set over medium-high heat. Bring just to the boiling point.
4. Purée the cooled sauce in a food processor or with an immersion blender in the pot. Whisk in the ketchup until fully combined.
5. Using a jar lifter, remove the hot jars from the canner and place on top of a kitchen cloth on the counter. With the help of a canning funnel, pack the blueberry ketchup into the jars, reserving ¼ inch headspace.
6. Use a spatula or wooden chopstick to remove any trapped air bubbles around the interior circumference of the jars. Wipe the rims clean with a damp cloth. Place on the lids and screw bands, tightening only until fingertip-tight.
7. Again using a jar lifter, slowly place the filled jars in the canner. Be sure that the jars are covered by at least 1 inch of water. Bring to a boil, and then process for 10 minutes, starting the timer once the water is at a full, rolling boil. Adjust for altitude as needed (see page 9 for detailed canning instructions).

MEATLOAF WITH KETCHUP CRUST

· SERVES 4 TO 6 ·

For me, meatloaf ranks mighty high in the pantheon of supreme comfort foods. I find it deeply satisfying, especially when served alongside piping hot, heavily buttered mashed potatoes. If the weather calls for snow, be sure to have these ingredients on hand. Enjoying a piece of this meatloaf when the world slowly turns white outside is one of my biggest, simplest joys.

2 strips Bacon (page 176)	Freshly ground black pepper
1 large onion, diced	3 eggs
3 garlic cloves, minced	Dash of hot sauce
1¼ cups Ketchup	2 cups breadcrumbs
1 cup milk	3 pounds lean ground beef
1 tablespoon sea salt	

1. Preheat the oven to 375°F and lightly oil a large rimmed baking sheet.
2. Warm a large pot or Dutch oven over medium heat. Add the bacon and cook until crispy. Set aside the bacon on a plate covered with a paper towel, leaving the grease behind in the pot.
3. Add the onion to the pot. Sauté for about 10 minutes, until the onion begins to brown around the edges. Add the garlic and cook for 2 more minutes. Stir in ¼ cup of the ketchup. Stir in the milk, a splash at a time. Stir in the salt and a few grinds of pepper.
4. Crumble the bacon and stir it in. Remove the pot from the heat.
5. Whisk the eggs and hot sauce in a medium bowl until fully incorporated. Stir the eggs into the mixture in the pot. Fold in the breadcrumbs and the beef. Stir until all the ingredients are well combined.
6. Form the mixture into a loaf, about 1½ inches thick, on the prepared baking sheet. Spread the remaining 1 cup ketchup evenly across the top. Cook for 50 minutes. Place under the broiler for 2 to 4 minutes, until the crust starts to brown a little. Allow the meatloaf to rest a few minutes before serving.

FRUITS
— & —
VEGETABLES

FERMENTED CABBAGE (SAUERKRAUT)

Preserving foods via fermentation has been practiced in the South for centuries. The Eastern Cherokee, residents of the mountains of western North Carolina, have been consuming a fermented corn soup known as "ganahena" or "connohanney" for as long as they have called the area home. Though fermentation traditions abound across the South, they do seem to be particularly well represented in the mountains of the Southern Appalachians. I have heard mention of everything from corncobs to beans being fermented in Henry County, Virginia, the native grounds of the maternal side of my family.

Fermenting through salt brining is how sauerkraut, or fermented cabbage, is created. According to food writer and North Carolina–based artisan food business Farmer's Daughter owner April McGreger, Palinate and Moravian German settlers likely introduced this means of food preservation to the Southeast. Creating communities across the Blue Ridge Mountains, as well as in the Piedmont and eastern parts of North Carolina, in addition to South Carolina, Georgia, Louisiana, and Texas, permitted the spread of salt brining fermentation throughout the South.

I didn't grow up with sauerkraut (my mom wasn't too keen on the stuff), but I am deeply fond of its long and storied history in the Southern Appalachian culinary canon. I've been enjoying it now for nearly two decades, and it's become my favorite fermented food. This recipe is from my close friend Adriana, who also generously provided the recipe for Fermented Hot Sauce (page 97). Adriana became interested in fermented foods several years ago, and began studying them in earnest, including a weeklong workshop with Sandor Katz, the fermentation guru, as it were, of our generation.

SERVING SUGGESTIONS
- *Serve warmed on a hot dog topped with a generous sprinkling of celery seeds and sea salt.*
- *You might think this sounds kooky, but a scattering of fermented cabbage is delicious on top of pizza.*
- *Use as a component of a tossed salad with roasted, salted sunflower seeds and homemade Thousand Island dressing.*

FERMENTED CABBAGE (SAUERKRAUT)

· MAKES 1 QUART ·

1 medium red or green cabbage
1 tablespoon sea salt

1. Tear off the outermost leaves of the cabbage and set them aside. Place the head of cabbage on a cutting board, and slice it into quarters. Remove and set aside the core pieces. Cut each quarter into very thin ribbons. Place in a nonreactive bowl such as glass, ceramic, or stainless steel.

2. Sprinkle the salt over the cabbage. Using clean hands, begin to massage and squeeze the cabbage. Continue for the next 5 to 10 minutes, until the cabbage ribbons move from dry and firm to limp and watery and begin to release water.

3. Transfer the mixture to a clean quart Mason jar. Pack it down until all of the mixture is in the jar. Make your hand into a fist and mash it down until water is released and covers the top of the cabbage pieces. Cover the cabbage with one of the outer leaves removed earlier, tucking it down into the sides of the jar.

4. Fill a half-pint jar with water. Secure a lid firmly atop it. Place this jar into the open quart jar, to serve as a weight during fermentation.

5. Place a kitchen cloth over the top of the weighted down quart jar and secure it with a rubber band. Store at room temperature out of direct sunlight.

6. Over the next 3 days, press down on the lid of the half-pint jar twice daily, to ensure that the cabbage remains submerged in its juices. If after the first 24 hours of fermentation, the cabbage isn't fully covered with liquid, dissolve 2 teaspoons of sea salt in a cup of cold water and pour in enough just to cover the cabbage. If any white bloom develops at the top of the liquid, simply scrape it off. If any colored mold appears, your batch is likely compromised and it's best to discard or compost this batch and begin anew.

7. Begin tasting after 3 days. If you like the taste and texture of the sauerkraut at this time, remove the smaller jar, cover the quart jar with a lid, and transfer to the refrigerator. If you prefer a stronger taste and/or more flaccid texture, continue fermenting the sauerkraut, tasting it daily until the flavor and texture is to your liking.

8. Store the sauerkraut in the refrigerator and use within 1 to 2 months.

SOUTHERN REUBEN

· SERVES 4 ·

I have never met a Reuben I didn't like. Even when I was vegetarian for fourteen years—and vegan for four before that—I still enjoyed Reubens (albeit tempeh offerings). This version swaps in ham, the most ubiquitous meat of the South, for corned beef, and hoop or cheddar cheese for Swiss. It's especially delicious with a crisp hard cider, such as from my longtime friend Trevor Baker's Asheville-based Noble Cider.

FOR THE MUSTARD SAUCE

1 cup mayonnaise

½ cup Sweet Pickle Relish (page 30)

3 tablespoons prepared brown mustard

1 teaspoon granulated garlic

FOR THE SANDWICHES

Butter, room temperature (page 194)

8 slices rye bread

Hoop or cheddar cheese

Thin ham slices

Fermented Cabbage (Sauerkraut)

1. Combine the mayonnaise, sweet pickle relish, brown mustard, and garlic in a small bowl. Mix until everything is fully incorporated.
2. Lightly butter one side of each slice of bread. Flip the bread over, and spread 1 to 2 tablespoons of mustard sauce on the insides. Layer the cheese, ham, and sauerkraut on top of the sauce in portions according to your liking.
3. Grill on the stovetop or press the sandwiches in a panini press until the cheese is melty. Serve immediately.
4. Store any unused mustard sauce in the refrigerator and use within 2 to 3 weeks.

BRATS WITH ONIONS, APPLES & KRAUT

· SERVES 4 ·

We eat brats a lot in our house. Several local farms produce delicious offerings, and our son Huxley enjoys them just as much as we do. Served with warm sauerkraut, apples, and onions, this makes for a satisfying meal on a brisk autumn evening or snowy winter's day.

1½ pounds brats

1 tablespoon Bacon Drippings (page 176)

1 onion, diced

One 12-ounce bottle hard cider or fresh apple cider

3 firm apples, peeled and diced

3 cups Fermented Cabbage (Sauerkraut)

1 teaspoon mustard seeds

1 teaspoon caraway seeds

1 teaspoon celery seeds

Rye toast, prepared brown mustard, and cheese, to serve (optional)

1. Pierce the brats several times with a fork. Warm a large pan or Dutch oven over medium heat. Add the bacon drippings. Once melted, sauté the brats for about 10 minutes, until evenly browned. Remove the brats from the pan, leaving about 2 tablespoons of grease behind.
2. Add the onion to the pan and sauté for about 10 minutes, until browned around the edges. Add the cider, apples, and sauerkraut, reduce the heat to low, and simmer for 5 minutes.
3. Slice the brats into bite-size pieces, and stir them into the pan. Simmer for 30 to 40 minutes, stirring occasionally, until there is no longer liquid pooling on the bottom of the pan.
4. Toast the mustard, caraway, and celery seeds in a small skillet or pan over medium heat for 1 to 2 minutes, until they become aromatic and several seeds begin to pop. Remove the pan from the heat.
5. Stir the seeds into the brats and simmer for 3 to 4 minutes. Remove the pan from the heat and serve immediately, with rye toast, brown mustard, and cheese of your choice, if desired.

CANNED TOMATOES

When I began outlining the "no compromise" recipes I would undoubtedly include in this book, canned tomatoes topped the list. Both how frequently I use them in my own kitchen and just how commonly they appear in beloved dishes across the Southern culinary landscape made it a foregone conclusion that canned tomatoes are a key component of any Southern pantry.

After Spanish colonists brought tomatoes to the New World via the Caribbean, tomato cultivation and production spread across the southern United States, with growers and packers commercially offering countless pounds of the fruits annually. Even in the mountains of North Carolina, the valleys are awash with tomato fields from May to late autumn.

Putting up jars of canned tomatoes is one of my favorite canning activities. If you have access to garden fresh tomatoes, either from your own garden or a local farm, use them. The flavor of your jarred tomatoes will be incomparable, and your winter self will thank you for your foresight and the generosity of your summertime labors.

SERVING SUGGESTIONS

- *Cooked tomatoes take on the volatile oils of any herbs they're cooked with, which makes them a key component in marinara sauce.*
- *Minestrone with homemade canned tomatoes is delicious beyond description (pro tip: use Pork Stock, page 187, to further intensify the flavor of the soup!).*
- *Chop zucchini, fresh peppers, and eggplant, and simmer slowly with fresh herbs and canned tomatoes for an easy ratatouille.*

CANNED TOMATOES

· MAKES 6 PINTS ·

---

8 pounds Roma, San Marzano, Jersey Giant, or Amish Paste tomatoes	6 tablespoons bottled lemon juice
	6 teaspoons sea salt

1. Rinse the tomatoes in cold water. Using a pointy tip knife, make a small crosshatch score across the bottom of each fruit. Fill a large metal bowl with ice water, and place it in the sink.

2. Bring a large pot of water to a boil over high heat. Drop the tomatoes into the boiling water for 30 to 60 seconds, until their skins split. Using a slotted spoon, remove the tomatoes from the pot and drop them into the reserved ice water bath. Once the tomatoes are cool enough to handle, slip off their skins.

3. Cut out the cores and roughly chop the tomatoes, retaining as much of their juices as possible (discard or compost the cores). Place the chopped tomatoes and all of their juices in a large pot or Dutch oven. Bring to a boil over high heat and then reduce to low. Simmer for 25 to 30 minutes, stirring frequently, until the juices begin to thicken a bit.

4. During the last 20 minutes of cooking time, fill a canner or large stockpot with water, place six pint jars inside, and set over medium-high heat. Bring just to the boiling point.

5. Using a jar lifter, remove the hot jars from the canner and place on top of a kitchen cloth on the counter. Add 1 tablespoon of lemon juice and 1 teaspoon of salt to each jar. With the help of a canning funnel, pack the chopped tomatoes into the jars, reserving ½ inch headspace.

6. Use a spatula or wooden chopstick to remove any trapped air bubbles around the interior circumference of the jars. Wipe the rims clean with a damp cloth. Place on the lids and screw bands, tightening only until fingertip-tight.

7. Again using a jar lifter, slowly place the filled jars in the canner. Be sure that the jars are covered by at least 1 inch of water. Bring to a boil, and then process for 45 minutes, starting the timer once the water is at a full, rolling boil. Adjust for altitude as needed (see page 9 for detailed canning instructions).

BRUNSWICK STEW

· SERVES 6 TO 8 ·

A thick, robust, meat and vegetable dish, my mom would call this a true "stick to your ribs" food. Packed with ingredients, the finished stew contains very little liquid, hence constituting it as a stew and not a soup. Regional variations abound throughout the South; this is my take on a Southern classic.

---

2 tablespoons extra-virgin olive oil

2 tablespoons Butter (page 194)

1 pound medium starch potatoes such as Yukon Gold, Kennebec, or Red, diced

2 carrots, diced

2 stalks celery, diced

1 large onion, diced

1 bell pepper (any color), diced

3 garlic cloves, minced

1 pint (2 cups) Canned Tomatoes

4 cups Chicken Stock (page 187)

1 cup Barbeque Sauce (page 94)

Meat from 1 whole cooked chicken, pulled from the bone and roughly chopped

1 pound Pulled Pork (page 95)

Hot sauce

1 pound cooked corn

1 pound cooked lima beans

Smoked or plain sea salt

1. Warm a large pot or Dutch oven over medium heat. Add the olive oil and butter. Once melted, add the potatoes, carrots, celery, onion, and bell pepper. Sauté over low heat, stirring frequently, for about 30 minutes, until the vegetables turn a bit brown around the edges.

2. Add the minced garlic and stir gently for 2 minutes. Add the tomatoes, stock, barbeque sauce, chicken, pork, and several dashes of hot sauce. Simmer on low heat for 30 minutes.

3. Stir in the corn and lima beans. Add salt to taste and serve immediately.

SOUTHERN SHAKSHUKA WITH HOECAKES

· SERVES 4 ·

A North African dish of eggs poached in a tomato sauce, shakshuka is intended to be eaten with bread right out of the pan, typically pita. My version uses hoecakes, a cornmeal flatbread that was a dietary staple of early settlers. The mythology surrounding their name purports slaves used to cook them on field hoes. Whatever the truth may be, hoecakes are a perfect means of scooping up this delicious tomato-based egg dish, an ideal meal at any time of day.

2 tablespoons extra-virgin olive oil

1 onion, diced

1 bell pepper, diced

3 garlic cloves, minced

2 pints (4 cups) Canned Tomatoes

2 teaspoons sea salt

2 teaspoons smoked paprika

1 teaspoon rubbed sage

1 teaspoon dried thyme

Freshly ground black pepper

Hot sauce

1 pound cooked black-eyed peas

1 pound cooked corn

8 eggs

¼ cup chopped parsley or cilantro, chopped

4 Pickled Okra, quartered (page 27)

4 ounces crumbled goat cheese

FOR THE HOECAKES

2 cups fine-grind cornmeal

1¼ cups boiling water

1 teaspoon sea salt

2 tablespoons Bacon Drippings (page 176)

1. Warm the olive oil over medium heat in a large stainless steel pan or enamel-coated cast iron skillet. Add the onion and pepper, and sauté for 10 minutes, until they start to brown around the edges and become fragrant and limp.
2. While the vegetables cook, prepare the hoecakes. Put the cornmeal, water, and salt in a medium bowl, stir to combine, and let rest for 10 minutes.
3. Stir the garlic into the onion mixture and cook for 2 minutes. Stir in the tomatoes, salt, paprika, sage, thyme, several grinds of pepper, and hot sauce to taste. Simmer for 20 minutes, stirring occasionally to avoid sticking.
4. While the sauce cooks, continue the hoecakes. Form the dough into eight evenly sized balls. Warm a skillet over medium heat. Add the bacon drippings. Once melted, pat the dough balls into 2- to 3-inch circles and fry in batches until golden and crispy on each side. Remove from the heat and set aside in an oven on the "warming" setting or at its lowest temperature.
5. Add the black-eyed peas to the sauce. Cook for 5 minutes and then add the corn. Cook for 5 minutes longer, stirring occasionally.
6. Crack the eggs into separate small bowls, without breaking their yolks. Stir the sauce and then use a large spoon to make seven evenly sized indentations across the surface of the sauce. Carefully pour the eggs into the indentations, and then cover the pan with a lid. Cook for 6 to 8 minutes, until the eggs are set.
7. Top with the fresh herbs, okra pickles, and crumbled goat cheese. Serve with the hoecakes and hot sauce on the side.

DRIED HOT PEPPERS

Native to the Americas and "discovered" by Spanish explorers in the New World, peppers are one hot commodity, if you'll permit my wretched and reprehensible use of puns. Covering a wide array of varietals, for the sake of ease, most spicy peppers are called "chili peppers" or "chilies" whereas the sweeter and mild types are bell peppers (or referred to by their color designations: green, red, yellow, purple, chocolate, or orange).

Peppers are an essential component of many Southern dishes. They grow well in this region, owing to the heat, sunshine, and relative humidity. From commercial operations to home gardeners, pretty much any type of pepper can be grown in the Southeast. Just down the road from me, Smoking J's Fiery Foods, a family-owned pepper farm, grows acres of hot and mild peppers, many of which are sold across the country.

The numerous ways to dry peppers include ovens set on low temperatures, dehydrators, as well as other more convoluted and involved techniques. My decidedly low-fi method requires merely a kitchen counter, a baking sheet, a cooling rack, and a dry, sunny spot, things all kitchens should be able to accommodate.

SERVING SUGGESTIONS

- *The heat in dried peppers, or any hot pepper for that matter, is great at breaking up mucus and phlegm. Add to chicken soup for heat when your household has the sniffles to clear up sinus congestion.*
- *Grind up and sprinkle over pizza, just like the tableside condiment at pizzerias.*
- *Use as a flavoring component in fra diavolo sauce.*
- *Crumble into lasagna layers alongside the ricotta.*

DRIED HOT PEPPERS

· AMOUNT VARIES ·

Any variety and any amount of hot peppers

1. Begin by inspecting each pepper. If you see any mushy or visibly spoiled spots, white spots, or diseased spots, discard those peppers.
2. Remove and discard or compost the peppers' stems. Wash the peppers in warm water and dry thoroughly with a kitchen cloth.
3. Place a metal cooling rack over a large rimmed baking sheet. Arrange the peppers in a single layer and set the pan in a dry, warm, sunny area.
4. Leave to dry for several weeks, flipping the peppers regularly and removing any that show signs of spoilage or softening. On days when the weather is sunny and warm, place the pan outdoors.
5. Once the peppers become dry and brittle, transfer them to an airtight lidded container. Store at room temperature out of direct sunlight and use within 1 to 2 years.

HOT PEPPER VINEGAR

· MAKES 1 PINT ·

Over the course of my life, at pretty much any Southern foods restaurant I have patronized across the Southeast, a jar of hot pepper vinegar could be found on the table. It is profoundly easy to make, so if you have a hot pepper lover in your house, or are one yourself, whip up a batch of this vinegar, stat.

Dried Hot Peppers   ½ teaspoon sea salt
½ to 1 cup Apple Cider Vinegar (page 88)

1. Fill a pint jar with the peppers.
2. Bring the vinegar and salt to a boil in a small pot over high heat. Boil for 2 minutes. Remove the pan from the heat and set aside to cool for 10 minutes.
3. Pour the vinegar over the peppers. Once the vinegar has fully cooled to room temperature, cover the jar with a lid. Store at room temperature out of direct sunlight.
4. For the next 3 weeks, give the jar a gentle shake daily. At the end of the infusing time, strain off the hot peppers. Transfer the vinegar to a wine bottle and cap it with a bar pour spout for easy pouring. Use within 6 months.

SMOKY & SPICY CHEESE STRAWS

· MAKES ABOUT 2½ TO 3 DOZEN ·

Next to the ham hock, I'd argue that cheese straws qualify as the culinary mascot of the South. They are featured at nearly every holiday and cocktail party, their secret recipe often carefully guarded by the host. I'm happy to share, though, as their deliciousness ought not be hidden away. You will need a cookie press to make these. Easily found at kitchen supply stores or online, they can be used to make shaped cookies when not making cheese straws.

1½ cups all-purpose flour

1 teaspoon smoked or plain sea salt

½ teaspoon smoked paprika

¼ teaspoon ground Dried Peppers

½ pound grated sharp cheddar cheese, room temperature

½ cup Butter, room temperature (page 194)

Several dashes of hot sauce

1. Whisk together the flour, salt, paprika, and ground peppers in a medium mixing bowl. Line a large rimmed baking sheet with a silicone baking mat or parchment paper.

2. Using an electric mixer, beat the cheese, butter, and hot sauce until light and fluffy, 4 to 5 minutes.

3. On low speed, gradually beat in the flour mixture just until the dough holds together and the ingredients are fully combined. The mixture will initially be grainy, but will eventually come together.

4. Preheat the oven to 350°F. Leave the dough to rest while the oven heats.

5. In batches, transfer the dough to a cookie press fitted with the star disk. Press the dough out in 4-inch pieces onto the prepared baking sheet. Repeat until all the dough has been pressed into straws.

6. Bake for 25 to 30 minutes, until the straws are lightly browned. Remove the pan from the oven. Cool in the pan for 5 minutes, and then transfer to a cooling rack. Cool for 20 minutes before serving. Store any unused cheese straws in a lidded airtight container and consume within 2 to 3 days.

CANNED STONE FRUITS

If you spend any appreciable amount of time in the South, you'll quickly learn just how sweet Southerners like their foods and beverages. From sweet tea to sweet pickles, from pecan pie to banana pudding, the South arguably keeps itself running on sugar. While I inherited my family's fondness for sweets, I didn't inherit it fully. Which is to say, I prefer my tea unsweetened (sacrilege!), and my desserts not too tremendously sweet.

One of my regular means of imbuing foods with a bit of sweetness is by using canned stone fruits. Preserved at the peak of ripeness, when their natural sugars are at their maximum potential, canned stone fruits enliven sweet and savory dishes with a kiss of sweetness, instead of a smack upside the head. Turning to them, instead of the sugar bowl or honey pot, allows me to craft delicious, Southern dishes while still being mindful of healthy eating.

When I think of my grandmother Nanny's pantry shelves, orbs of peaches suspended in syrup come to the forefront of my recollection. Although summer stone fruits are fleeting in the season, you can enjoy them year-round when canned and stored for later use. This syrup is a light one, as I don't prefer a cloyingly sweet taste. If you like yours sweeter (as Nanny certainly did), feel free to double or triple the sugar.

SERVING SUGGESTIONS

- *Neutral-tasting meats pair well with the sweetness of fruits. Chop some canned peaches, cherries, or apricots into bite-size pieces, stir into mayonnaise, and use as a spread for ham or turkey sandwiches. A scattering of minced fresh basil or mint further heightens the fruit's flavors.*
- *Pour about ¼ cup into a medium bowl and serve with cottage cheese for a midday snack.*
- *Warm and serve with Layer Cake (page 233) and homemade whipped cream.*

CANNED STONE FRUITS

· MAKES 4 PINTS ·

---

4 pounds ripe cherries (pitted and left whole), nectarines (pitted and left in halves), apricots (pitted and left in halves), or peaches (peeled, pitted, and left in halves)

1 cup sugar

3 cups water

1. Prep the fruit or fruits of your choice according to the ingredient list.
2. Fill a canner or large stockpot with water, place four pint jars inside, and set over medium-high heat. Bring just to the boiling point.
3. Stir the sugar and water in a medium saucepan over medium heat until all the sugar crystals are dissolved. Raise the heat to high and boil for 5 minutes. Remove from the heat.
4. Using a jar lifter, remove the hot jars from the canner and place on top of a kitchen cloth on the counter. With the help of a canning funnel, pack fruit into each jar, and then pour the sugar water on top, reserving ½ inch headspace for both fruit and sugar water.

5. Use a spatula or wooden chopstick to remove any trapped air bubbles around the interior circumference of the jars. Wipe the rims clean with a damp cloth. Place on the lids and screw bands, tightening only until fingertip-tight.

6. Again using a jar lifter, slowly place the filled jars in the canner. Be sure that the jars are covered by at least 1 inch of water. Bring to a boil, and then process for 10 minutes, starting the timer once the water is at a full, rolling boil. Adjust for altitude as needed (see page 9 for detailed canning instructions).

MUSCADINE, PEACH & HERB GELATIN SALAD
· SERVES 6 TO 8 ·

More of a palate cleanser than a sweet dessert, this gelatin salad is my version of the wobbly, fruit-filled salads offered on pretty much every salad bar in the South. I use muscadine grape juice here, as the grapes are ubiquitous in the region. Feel free to swap in Concord or white grape juice.

1 pint (2 cups) Canned Peaches

1 tablespoon minced fresh basil

1 tablespoon minced fresh mint

4 envelopes plain gelatin

1 cup muscadine, Concord, or white grape juice, chilled

3 cups muscadine, Concord, or white grape juice, heated

1. Combine the peaches, basil, and mint in a medium mixing bowl. Pour into a gelatin mold or Bundt pan.

2. In a heatproof bowl, sprinkle the gelatin over the cold grape juice. Let rest for 1 minute.

3. Whisk in the hot grape juice and stir until the gelatin completely dissolves, about 5 minutes.

4. Pour the mixture over the fruit and herbs. Place in the refrigerator and chill until completely set, at least 4 hours.

5. To serve, dip the tip of a sharp knife into cold water. Use the tip to carefully loosen the gelatin from the sides of the mold or Bundt pan. Dip the bottom and sides of the pan into warm (not hot) water for about 5 seconds. Place a serving plate on the top of the pan. Holding both the plate and pan together firmly, flip them over, so that the plate is on the bottom and the pan is on top. Give the pan a firm shake, so that the gelatin slips out of the pan and onto the serving plate. Serve immediately.

PORK TENDERLOIN WITH CHERRY & DRIED FRUIT COMPOTE

An excellent means of using up canned cherries (you can only put so many on sundaes, after all!), this pork tenderloin is exactly what you want when the mercury dips and it's dark out at 5:30 in the evening. It would make a lovely Christmas Eve or New Year's Eve entrée, as well.

1½ pound pork tenderloin, cut in half

1 teaspoon sea salt

Freshly ground black pepper

2 teaspoons Lard (page 173)

1 cup red wine

1 pint (2 cups) Canned Cherries, drained and liquid reserved

½ cup Dried Apples, diced (page 132)

½ cup golden raisins

¼ cup dried currants or raisins

1. Sprinkle the meat with the salt and several grinds of pepper. Place on a large plate or platter and let rest at room temperature for at least 5 minutes.

2. Warm the lard in a large saucepan over medium-high heat. Add the meat and brown, turning every minute, for 10 minutes.

3. Turn the heat down to low and add the wine and reserved cherry liquid. Braise the meat, turning every couple of minutes, for 20 minutes.

4. Add the cherries, apples, raisins, and currants. Cook for 7 to 9 minutes, until the center of the meat is at least 145°F and the liquid is almost all cooked off.

5. Remove the pork from the pan, transfer it onto a cutting board, and let it rest for 10 minutes. Slice into medallions.

6. Gently rewarm the fruit in the pan. Plate the meat, and spoon the fruit over it. Serve immediately.

DRIED APPLES

My mom has an extremely prolific and generous apple tree in her front yard in Burnsville, North Carolina. She does nothing to it, and yet, year after year, it bestows more apples than she or I will ever use. After I've made my fill of applesauce, apple butter, and more, I start drying them. Dried apples are an excellent snack when afternoon munchies strike when paired with some sharp cheddar cheese and a handful of pecans.

One town over from Mom's place is the adorable mountain hamlet of Spruce Pine. Along its main street, a train rumbles through on the regular, flanked by the Toe River on the other side. Though it's roughly an hour and a half away from our house, we frequently go to Spruce Pine simply to enjoy its mountain charm.

Just up the road from downtown Spruce Pine, you'll find the Orchard at Altapass. Built in 1908 by the Clinchfield Railroad, this 110-year-old orchard/Appalachian Cultural Center is a refuge in the clouds. Alongside tasty specimens of apples you'll find a celebration of the rich fabric of culture that comprises the Blue Ridge Mountains. Music, dancing, storytelling, foods, and pantry goods are all accounted for at Altapass. I've visited several times and always leave with a bag of apples destined to find a multitude of uses in my kitchen, including rendered into dried, delicious slices.

SERVING SUGGESTIONS

- *Chop into bite-size pieces and stir into zucchini bread, or bake with cranberries and toasted pecans into scones.*
- *Use in chicken salad for some sweetness and a bit of chewiness.*
- *Dried apple stack cakes have long been served in the Southern Appalachians on special occasions such as weddings and birthdays.*
- *Use as a component of a stuffing or dressing at Thanksgiving (or any time of year!).*

DRIED APPLES

· MAKES ABOUT 2 CUPS ·

4 apples (see Note)
Juice from 1 lemon

NOTE: I like my dried apples with their peels on, but you can feel free to peel your apples before you core them if you prefer.

1. Wash and inspect the apples. If any are too riddled with holes from insects or severely bruised, set them aside for the compost pile and choose others instead.
2. Core the apples, and then slice them into ¼-inch-thick rings.
3. Make a solution in a large glass or ceramic bowl of the lemon juice and enough cold water to cover the apple rings.
4. Add the apple rings and soak for 15 minutes. Transfer to wire cake cooling racks or a perforated pizza pan.
5. Place in an oven set to the lowest setting. Warm for 3 hours.
6. The rings should have the feel of soft, pliant leather when properly dried. They should be flexible but not have a tacky or watery feel. If you'd like them more crisp, feel free to pop them back in the oven for a bit, but take care not to over-dry them; doing so prevents them from storing well.
7. Store in an airtight container and consume within 1 to 2 months.

APPALACHIAN PLOUGHMAN'S LUNCH

· AMOUNT VARIES ·

A Ploughman's lunch is one of my favorite ways of eating. Akin to a Mediterranean mezze, a whole "mess" of items, to use the Southern parlance, are spread across the table, encouraging nibbling, snacking, and general feasting.

Loaf of crusty bread
Butter, room temperature (page 194)
Peach Chutney (page 74)
Sharp cheddar cheese
Thick slices of sweet ham
Fresh apples, sliced

Dried Apples
Pickled Eggs (page 56)
Sweet Onion Relish (page 35)
Pickled Okra (page 27)
Pickled Beets (page 24)
Bread & Butter Pickles (page 22)

1. Arrange portions of all the items on a cutting board.
2. Cut thick slices of bread and top with butter or chutney, cheddar cheese, and ham. Serve with the other items on the side.

FENNEL & DRIED APPLE GRANOLA

· MAKES 4 CUPS ·

Homemade granola is a deeply economical, satisfying, nourishing breakfast or snack. Aside from its cost-saving abilities, what I especially love about homemade granola is the ability to customize its flavor and ingredients to your liking (that's what DIY is all about anyway, right?!). I use fennel seeds in this recipe, but if licoricey notes aren't to your liking, feel free to swap with ground cloves, ginger, allspice, or cardamom.

1½ cups rolled oats

½ cup whole almonds, toasted

¼ cup pumpkin seeds, toasted

¼ cup sunflower seeds, toasted

½ cup unsweetened dried coconut flakes

¼ cup honey

¼ cup extra-virgin olive oil

2 tablespoons light brown sugar

1 teaspoon ground cinnamon

1 teaspoon fennel seeds

½ teaspoon sea salt

½ cup Dried Apples, chopped (page 132)

1. Preheat the oven to 300°F. Oil a large rimmed baking sheet.

2. Place the oats, almonds, pumpkin seeds, sunflower seeds, coconut, honey, olive oil, brown sugar, cinnamon, fennel seeds, and salt in a large bowl. Stir with a mixing spoon to coat completely.

3. Spread the mixture evenly onto the prepared baking sheet. Bake for 35 to 40 minutes, stirring every 10 minutes, until lightly browned and fragrant.

4. Remove the baking sheet from the oven and let cool for 10 minutes. Transfer the granola to a large mixing bowl and stir in the dried apples. Store in an airtight container and use within 3 to 4 weeks.

5

DRY GOODS
— & —
SUNDRIES

GRITS

A Native American dish, grits are made from hominy, which is corn that has been soaked in lye to remove the outer husk, and then ground into a coarse meal. The meal is then cooked in liquid, and seasoned with salt and, historically, an animal fat. It is the inclusion of that fat, I feel, that really differentiates good grits from grits. Without a bit of butter, or even bacon grease, grits fall flat, with relatively little satiating mouthfeel or flavor to speak of.

I honestly cannot tell you how many non-Southerners, and even some Southerners, have told me they don't like grits. Whenever I hear this, I reply immediately with "Oh, but you haven't had MY grits." The thing is, most people have never had grits prepared properly. The quick grits attempting to pass themselves off as the real deal are utterly lacking in the flavor complexity of their whole grain cousins. They're also served terribly runny, only exacerbating their unappealing nature. Furthermore, most prepared grits are cooked with water and water only.

I didn't grow up on grits. My mother was one of those Southerners wholly convinced she didn't like them. I had a feeling she would, though, if I could only make them appetizing. After much trial and error, and lots of grits that just didn't make the cut, I came up with this recipe. I have served these grits to at least five "anti-grits" people who became converts at first taste. Try my grits and see what a difference the right ingredients and the right preparation makes.

SERVING SUGGESTIONS

- *Grits are highly versatile, serving as a creamy base for countless flavor pairings. Determine if you're in the mood for sweet or savory and use that as your launching point.*
- *Serve with Country Ham & Applesauce (page 105) for a hearty breakfast.*
- *Drizzle with maple syrup and top with fresh fruit for a morning or mid-day snack.*
- *Top with a poached egg, wilted spinach, and fresh basil pieces.*
- *Cover with shredded cheddar or hoop cheese and crumbled Bacon (page 176).*

GRITS

· MAKES ABOUT 4 CUPS ·

2 cups cold water

2 cups whole milk

1 teaspoon sea salt

1 cup corn grits

4 tablespoons Butter, room temperature
(page 194)

1. Combine the water, milk, salt, and grits in a medium heavy-bottomed pot. Stir to ensure all ingredients are fully combined. Bring to a boil over medium-high heat.
2. Cover the pot and reduce the heat to a simmer. Cook for 25 minutes, stirring occasionally.
3. Remove from the heat and add the butter. Replace the lid and let sit for 5 minutes, then stir until creamy. Serve immediately.

SHRIMP & GRITS BUFFET

· SERVES 4 TO 6 ·

One day, in a moment of sheer brilliance, my husband, Glenn, had the idea to create a kind of grits smorgasbord. Calling it "Pimpin' Grits," I prepared a huge batch of grits while we cooked up loads of shrimp. Friends provided all the other ingredients, potluck-style. What's so lovely about dining this way is that, no matter what type of diet you maintain—carnivore, vegetarian, gluten-free—this buffet satisfies just about everyone. A dinner table where everyone's needs are met is one I want to be seated at, to be sure!

1 tablespoon extra-virgin olive oil

1½ pounds large shrimp, peeled and deveined (shrimp shells reserved)

4 cups water

4 strips Bacon (page 176)

1 sweet onion, diced

2 stalks celery, diced

1 red bell pepper, diced

3 garlic cloves, minced

4 tablespoons Butter (page 194)

1 cup rosé or white wine

1 tablespoon Worcestershire sauce

Dash of hot sauce

1 teaspoon sea salt

4 cups cooked Grits

Optional toppings: grated hoop cheese, fresh chopped cilantro, crumbled country ham, grilled carrots, roasted tomatoes, chopped pimentos, sliced radishes, spicy corn relish, grilled hot peppers, roasted corn, crispy fried sage leaves, and hot sauce

1. Warm the olive oil in a medium saucepan over medium heat. Setting the peeled shrimp aside, add the shrimp shells, toss to coat, and cook for about 3 minutes, until pink. Add the water, reduce the heat to low, and simmer until about one-third of the liquid remains. Drain off the shrimp shells and set aside the stock. Discard the shrimp shells.

2. Return the pan to the heat, increase it to medium-high, and add the bacon. Cook until lightly crispy, then transfer to a plate lined with a paper towel.

3. Add the onion, celery, and bell pepper to the bacon grease left in the pan. Sauté for about 15 minutes, until the vegetables are browned around the edges. While the vegetables cook, crumble the cooked bacon.

4. Add the garlic and cook, stirring for 2 minutes. Add the butter and melt it entirely. Add the wine, reserved shrimp stock, crumbled bacon, Worcestershire sauce, hot sauce, and salt. Cook down the liquid for about 20 minutes, until about one-third remains in the pan.

5. Stir in the shrimp and simmer for a few minutes, until cooked through.

6. Serve immediately over hot grits, with any combination of toppings.

SERAFINA'S CHICKEN & GRITS

· SERVES 6 ·

I participate in an all-women "Feel Good Book Club" (referring to how we feel when we're all together, not necessarily the content of the books we select) with meetings that incorporate a pot-luck meal based on that month's selection. In August 2016 we were lucky enough to be joined by Asheville, North Carolina–based young adult fiction author Robert Beatty, and his wife, Jennifer, to chat about Robert's *New York Times* best-selling book, *Serafina and the Black Cloak*. Central to the book's theme is a simple meal of chicken and grits that Serafina's "Pa" regularly prepares. I'd learned through Beatty's publicist that the author disliked grits, and I took on the challenge of serving him a version that he'd come to love. When he declared my grits to be the best he'd ever had, I knew this recipe was a winner. When he requested that I call my dish "Serafina's Chicken & Grits," I gladly accepted with more than a wee bit of pride.

4 tablespoons extra-virgin olive oil

3 pounds boneless, skinless chicken thighs

2 large onions, roughly chopped

1½ cups Chicken Stock (page 187)

1 tablespoon sugar

1 cup red wine or Concord grape juice

1 tablespoon Worcestershire sauce

1 teaspoon dried thyme

1 teaspoon dried sage

1 teaspoon sea salt

Freshly ground black pepper

4 cups cooked Grits

Pickled Okra slices, to serve, (optional; page 27)

Chopped fresh parsley and tarragon, to serve (optional)

1. Heat 2 tablespoons of the olive oil in a large pot or Dutch oven over medium heat. Cook the chicken for about 10 to 15 minutes, until browned all around the outside. Remove the chicken and juices from the pot, and set aside in a bowl.

2. Add the remaining 2 tablespoons olive oil to the pot. Add the onions and cook for 10 to 12 minutes, until browned around the edges.

3. Add 1 cup of the chicken stock, reduce the heat to low, and simmer for about 20 minutes, until the liquid is gone.

4. Stir in the remaining ½ cup chicken stock and the sugar. Simmer for 15 minutes until the liquid is gone and the onions are nicely caramelized.

5. Stir in the wine, Worcestershire sauce, thyme, sage, salt, and several grinds of pepper. Stir in the chicken and juices, and simmer for 5 minutes.

6. Transfer the contents of the pot to a slow cooker. Cook on low for 6 hours, stirring occasionally. When the chicken is done, remove the chicken and onions from the slow cooker.

7. Transfer the juices to a medium saucepan and reduce over medium heat for several minutes, until the liquid begins to thicken up. Stir in the chicken and onions, gently breaking up the chicken. Cook for 4 to 5 minutes. Remove the pan from the heat.

8. Serve over hot grits, topped with slices of pickled okra, parsley, and tarragon, if desired.

CORNBREAD

Versions of hot, corn-based breads were being baked on the continent well before European colonists arrived. "Suppone" and "pone" are but two names that Native Americans gave to their cornbreads, which consisted of ground cornmeal and liquid, typically water. Since then, additional ingredients have been introduced to lighten and leaven the bread, including fats (butter, bacon grease, vegetable oils), eggs, milk or buttermilk, and baking soda and baking powder.

I am deeply picky about cornbread. According to my standards, a properly prepared pan should possess no added sugar, have a moist interior and crumby exterior, and be simultaneously smoky, salty, and naturally sweet. It needs to be baked with bacon drippings and butter, and contain no trace of processed vegetable oils. While I welcome white or yellow cornmeal equally, so long as my other criteria are met, I do tend to gravitate toward yellow cornbread, as that is the kind I grew up eating.

Essentially, what I'm describing is my grandmother's cornbread, the kind she baked regularly, having learned from her own mother, my Mamaw. I would rather have no cornbread at all than one that is too sweet, or baked with vegetable oil, or so light and fluffy and devoid of exterior crunch that it might as well be a slice of cake. I tell you, when it comes to cornbread, I am Goldilocks. The side eye I give most cornbread would make a grown man cry. What I offer here is a version my ancestors would applaud.

SERVING SUGGESTIONS

- *Cornbread complements hearty, savory fare by imparting a bit of sweetness without adding to the meal's heaviness. Crumble into a bowl of all-beef or vegetarian chili.*
- *Use as the base for a dressing or stuffing. You could crumble some cooked Breakfast Sausage (page 182) into the stuffing; roasted chestnuts added to the mix would be delicious, too.*
- *Slather a wedge with Butter (page 194) and drizzle with sorghum syrup.*
- *Partner with Southern Pinto Beans (page 167) or Southern Greens with Chow Chow (page 20).*

CORNBREAD

· SERVES 6 TO 8 ·

---

6 tablespoons Butter (page 194)

2 tablespoons Bacon Drippings (page 176; see Note)

1¼ cups medium-grind yellow cornmeal

1 cup all-purpose flour

1 teaspoon baking soda

1 teaspoon sea salt

1½ cups Buttermilk, room temperature (page 199)

3 eggs, room temperature

NOTE: For a vegetarian version, replace the bacon grease with an equal amount of butter.

1. Preheat the oven to 400°F. Place the butter and bacon grease in a 9-inch cast iron skillet or pie pan. Put the pan in the oven, allowing the fats to melt and the pan to heat while you prepare the batter.
2. Sift together the cornmeal, flour, baking soda, and salt in a medium mixing bowl.
3. Whisk together the buttermilk and eggs in a large bowl. Remove the heated pan from the oven, and carefully pour all but several teaspoons of the melted fat into the bowl. Whisk until fully combined.
4. Whisk the dry ingredients into the wet, combining just until the batter is free of lumps.
5. Pour the batter into the heated pan. Bake for 20 to 25 minutes, until the top is golden brown and the sides of the cornbread begin to pull away from the edges of the pan. Cool for 10 to 15 minutes before serving.

KILT SPINACH SALAD WITH BACON VINAIGRETTE & CORNBREAD CROUTONS

· SERVES 4 ·

A kilt salad does not resemble or in any way share an affinity with a men's plaid skirt of the same name. What's being described is a warm salad in which the greens have been "kilt" or wilted by the addition of hot fat, and is a dish tied to the Southern Appalachians.

FOR THE CROUTONS

1 batch Cornbread, cut into bite-size cubes

¼ cup extra-virgin olive oil

½ teaspoon sea salt

FOR THE SPINACH

¾ cup extra-virgin olive oil

1 garlic clove, peeled and smashed

3 pieces Bacon, cooked until lightly crisped and crumbled (page 176)

1 tablespoon light brown sugar

½ teaspoon sea salt

Freshly ground black pepper

¼ cup white wine vinegar

10 ounces fresh spinach leaves

1. Preheat the oven to 400°F. Arrange the cornbread cubes evenly on a large rimmed baking sheet, with some space in between each cube.
2. Drizzle the cornbread with the olive oil, and then sprinkle evenly with the salt. Toss gently to coat and then spread out the cubes again on the baking sheet. Bake for 10 minutes. Remove the pan from the oven, gently flip the cubes, and bake for 8 minutes longer until crispy and golden. Remove the pan from the oven and set the croutons aside to cool while you prepare the spinach.
3. Warm the olive oil over low heat in a medium saucepan. Add the garlic, cook for 1 minute, and then remove the garlic from the pan.
4. Stir in the crumbled bacon, brown sugar, salt, and several grinds of pepper until fully incorporated, then turn off the heat. Let the mixture sit for 2 to 3 minutes and then carefully (it may splatter a little) stir in the vinegar.
5. Place the spinach in a medium heatproof bowl. Pour the dressing over the greens. Using salad tongs, toss the spinach with the dressing and serve immediately, topped with the cornbread croutons.

CORNBREAD SAUSAGE CASSEROLE

· SERVES 8 TO 10 ·

Casseroles are more than dishes for feeding a crowd. They're meals of comfort conveying a sense of love and care for the recipient. They travel well, and nourish heartily. A birth, a death, a convalescence, a pick-me-up, casseroles are greeting cards in edible form. This recipe is also wonderful for a simple weekend brunch at home.

2 pounds Breakfast Sausage (page 182)	Several dashes of hot sauce
1 medium onion, diced	1 teaspoon sea salt, plus a pinch for topping
1 bell pepper (any color), diced	Freshly ground black pepper
3 garlic cloves, minced	1 batch Cornbread, cut into bite-size cubes
1 pound cooked corn kernels	1 tablespoon Butter, melted (page 194)
8 eggs	1 teaspoon granulated garlic
2 cups Buttermilk (page 199)	

1. Liberally butter a 9 x 13-inch casserole pan. Set aside.

2. Warm a large pot or Dutch oven over medium heat. Add the sausage and brown for about 10 minutes, until cooked through. Scoop out the sausage into a fine-mesh sieve set atop a heat-proof jar or small bowl. Drain off any excess fat and discard (or give it to your dogs!). If any fat remains in the pot, remove all but 2 tablespoons.

3. Add the onion and bell pepper to the fat in the pan. Sauté for 10 minutes, until the vegetables start to brown slightly around the edges.

4. Add the garlic and cook, stirring for 2 minutes, then remove the pot from the heat. Stir the sausage and corn into the vegetable mix. Set aside. Preheat the oven to 350°F.

5. Whisk the eggs, buttermilk, hot sauce, salt, and a few grinds of pepper in a medium bowl until incorporated.

6. Gently toss three-quarters of the cornbread with the buttermilk mixture in a large mixing bowl, and then let sit for several minutes.

7. In a food processor, pulse the remaining cornbread with the melted butter, garlic, a pinch of salt, and a few grinds of pepper until uniform. This will be the topping. Set aside.

8. Gently toss the sausage and vegetable mixture with the cornbread and buttermilk mixture. Spread out into the buttered casserole pan. Sprinkle the topping evenly across the surface of the casserole.

9. Bake for 45 minutes, until the center is firm and the casserole is cooked throughout. Let cool for 20 to 30 minutes before serving.

BUTTERMILK BISCUITS

Biscuits have been consumed in the South for centuries. Early iterations, according to Nathalie Dupree and Cynthia Graubart in their book *Southern Biscuits*, were made solely of flour and water, essentially hardtack, able to withstand long travel. Over time, fats (such as lard, butter, and later, vegetable shortening or oil) and baking powder, a creation of the 1800s, were added to the mix.

These days, you won't find any hard and fast, definitive recipe for biscuit-making. There exist as many ways to make biscuits as there are means of consuming them. Some rise high from the pan while others are short little things. Some are ultra-crispy on the outside and others are moist throughout. Cut biscuits, drop biscuits, tiny biscuits. There is a biscuit for every need, persuasion, and inclination.

This biscuit recipe was born out of a deep desire to create my ideal specimen. I prefer a biscuit that is cut (as opposed to dropped), with sharp edges providing crispiness as well as evidence of flaky layers inside. I want my biscuits covered in melted butter just before baking, producing a top that is golden brown and offering a hit of fat and salt. The recipe makes a dozen smaller biscuits. If you want half as many large ones that you can fill with a fried egg, use a 3½-inch cutter.

SERVING SUGGESTIONS

- *The sour tang of buttermilk biscuits marries well with the rich unctuousness of gravies. Cover one or two with Sausage Gravy (page 185) for a rousing breakfast.*
- *Slather with Butter (page 194) and Muscadine Jelly (page 71).*
- *Use as a topping for a chicken potpie.*
- *Fry Breakfast Sausage (page 182) patties and use as a filling for a sausage biscuit. Spread on a little Hot Pepper Jelly (page 82) for some heat.*

BUTTERMILK BISCUITS

· MAKES ABOUT 1 DOZEN ·

2½ cups all-purpose flour

1 tablespoon baking powder

1 teaspoon sea salt

8 tablespoons cold Butter, cubed (page 194)

1 cup Buttermilk (page 199)

2 tablespoons Butter, melted, for the biscuit tops (page 194)

1. Preheat the oven to 425°F. Line a large rimmed baking sheet with parchment paper or a silicone baking mat. Set aside.
2. Whisk the flour, baking powder, and salt in a large mixing bowl until fully incorporated.
3. Using a pastry cutter or two forks, cut in the cold butter until the mixture begins to look crumbly but some pea-size chunks of butter still remain.

4. Make a well in the center of the flour mixture. Slowly add the buttermilk. Stir with a large spoon just until the liquid has been absorbed into the flour.

5. Dump the shaggy dough onto a lightly floured countertop. Knead the dough with your hands, pressing it over and onto itself about three times (this helps creates the flaky layers that form inside biscuits).

6. Use a rolling pin to flatten the dough to about ¾-inch thickness. With a 2½-inch biscuit cutter, cut out about twelve biscuits, re-rolling scraps of dough as necessary.

7. Transfer the biscuits to the prepared baking sheet. Using a pastry brush, brush the melted butter evenly over the tops of the biscuits.

8. Bake for 15 to 20 minutes, until the biscuits are golden brown. Remove from the oven and cool the biscuits on the sheet for 5 minutes before serving.

HAM BISCUIT WITH MUSTARD COMPOUND BUTTER

· MAKES 6 BISCUITS ·

Country ham biscuits are so deeply satisfying. Add in the sharpness of whole-grain mustard and you've got a breakfast biscuit that practically shouts "rise and shine!"

½ cup Butter, softened (page 194)

2 tablespoons whole-grain prepared mustard

12 ounces country ham

6 Buttermilk Biscuits (see Note)

NOTE: Substitute a 3½-inch size biscuit cutter for the 2½-inch size called for in the recipe. This will yield 6 large biscuits instead of a dozen small ones.

1. Stir together the butter and mustard until well combined.

2. In a cast iron skillet or large pan, fry the country ham over medium heat until cooked through.

3. Cut the biscuits in half and spread about 1 tablespoon of the mustard butter on each half.

4. Divide the country ham evenly between the biscuit halves, top with the other half, and serve immediately.

SOUTHERN BENEDICT

· SERVES 4 ·

My take on eggs Benedict gives the classic dish a Southern twist via biscuits, country ham, and fried eggs. For this rich dish, a little goes a long way. It would be lovely served alongside a salad of lightly dressed greens.

FOR THE HOLLANDAISE REMOULADE

8 tablespoons Butter (page 194)

3 egg yolks, room temperature

2 tablespoons water

2 tablespoons prepared whole-grain mustard

FOR THE BENEDICT

Pinch of sea salt

Freshly ground black pepper

Dash of hot sauce

1 tablespoon lemon juice

1 tablespoon dried tarragon, or 3 tablespoons finely chopped fresh tarragon

¼ cup cornichons or pickles

2 tablespoons capers

2 Buttermilk Biscuits

4 fried eggs

8 ounces country ham, fried

1. **PREPARE THE HOLLANDAISE.** Melt the butter in a small pan over low heat until bubbling. Transfer to a measuring cup with a spout.
2. Whisk the egg yolks with the water in a metal bowl. Place the bowl over a gently simmering pot of water, so that the bottom of the bowl is above the water, creating a double boiler.
3. Whisk constantly, adding the melted butter a little at a time, until fully blended and slightly thickened. Remove the bowl and pot from the heat, and then remove the bowl from the pot of water.
4. Stir the mustard, salt, several grinds of pepper, hot sauce, lemon juice, and tarragon into the bowl.
5. Chop the cornichons and capers into a fine relish. Stir into the sauce. If the sauce is too thick, thin it with a few drops of water.
6. Slice the biscuits in half. Place one biscuit half on each of the four plates. Top each biscuit with 2 ounces of country ham, followed by a fried egg. Drizzle the hollandaise remoulade evenly across the eggs. Serve immediately.

HUSHPUPPIES

As with other corn-based breads of the South, the roots of hushpuppies lie in Native American foodways. Cornbread, grits, hoecakes, spoonbread, corncakes—these all owe a debt of gratitude to the cultivation of corn in the Americas. By integrating new means of preparing cornmeal with existing traditions, a host of unique breads were created in the New World.

These days, you can find hushpuppies across the United States. Many would argue, however, that none are as good as those cooked in the Southern states. Carefully guarded "secret" recipes abound, writes John Egerton in *Southern Food*. As with biscuits, many iterations and permutations for hushpuppies exist. Whether to include scallions, scooped into rounds or shaped into tubes, fried in peanut oil, lard, or vegetable oil—all possible considerations in an individual cook's hushpuppy-making practices.

The mythology around hushpuppies is that cooks frying up cornmeal-battered foods would toss some to their dogs with an admonishment to "Hush, puppy!" to placate the hungry, barking pups. Whether or not that's true, I can testify to the power of well-executed hushpuppies to soothe the savage beast. I hope mine offer you more than a little bit of comfort. Be sure to use new, or nearly new, baking soda and baking powder when making hushpuppies. Using fresh leavening agents is key to their success.

SERVING SUGGESTIONS

- *Hushpuppies and Pulled Pork & Barbeque Sauce (page 95) are a Southern tradition, with the piquant flavor of the sauce cutting through the fat and oil of the puppies.*
- *The bold creaminess of Pimento Cheese (page 33) marries well with the sweet crunch of hushpuppies. Use as a dip.*
- *Serve alongside Buttermilk & Smoky Paprika Fried Chicken (page 200) and Russet Potato & Dilly Bean Salad (page 42).*

HUSHPUPPIES

· SERVES 6 TO 8 ·

1 cup fine-grind cornmeal

½ cup all-purpose flour

½ teaspoon baking soda

½ teaspoon baking powder

½ teaspoon sea salt

Freshly ground black pepper

1 egg, room temperature

1 cup Buttermilk, room temperature (page 199)

½ Vidalia onion, minced

2 tablespoons finely chopped chives

Peanut oil for frying

1. Whisk together the cornmeal, flour, baking soda, baking powder, salt, and several grinds of pepper in a medium mixing bowl. In a separate large bowl, whisk together the egg, buttermilk, onion, and chives.

2. Pour the dry mixture into the wet mixture, stirring just until all the ingredients are fully combined. Cover the bowl with a kitchen cloth and set aside to rest for 10 minutes.

3. Pour 3 inches of peanut oil into an electric fryer, stockpot, Dutch oven, or other high-sided pot. Heat the oil to between 350°F and 360°F and then hold the temperature steady in that range.

4. Using a small ice cream scoop or melon ball scoop, drop rounded tablespoons of the batter into the oil. Aim to fry batches of eight hushpuppies at a time.

5. Cook for 1 to 2 minutes, rotating the batter with kitchen tongs as soon as they begin to float. Once they're golden brown on all sides, use a kitchen spider or slotted spoon to transfer them to a plate lined with a paper towel. Repeat until you have fried all of the batter. Serve immediately.

CORNMEAL CATFISH WITH SPIKEY TARTAR SAUCE

· SERVES 4 ·

The fish fry is pretty ubiquitous across the South. When I spent time in Carteret County, North Carolina, during my junior and senior years of high school, I was always seeing a flyer or poster advertising an upcoming charitable event in the form of a fish fry. What distinguishes my fry, though, is a light coating of oil, not a full deep dive (that's reserved for the hushpuppies served alongside). And since hushpuppies and tartar sauce are as classic a combo as Fred and Ginger, Mickey and Minnie, and Dolly Parton and wigs, I'm also offering up a special sauce. This recipe makes more than you'll need for dipping into a batch, but will keep for some time, and can also make a lovely spread for deli meat sandwiches or even burgers.

FOR THE TARTAR SAUCE

1 cup mayonnaise

¼ cup Sweet Pickle Relish (page 30)

1 tablespoon prepared horseradish

1 tablespoon coarse-grain mustard

1 tablespoon lemon juice

Several dashes of hot sauce

FOR THE CORNMEAL CATFISH

½ cup medium-grind cornmeal

½ cup fine-grind cornmeal

1 tablespoon granulated garlic

1 teaspoon sea salt

Freshly ground black pepper

2 eggs

Dash of hot sauce

1½ pounds catfish fillets

Light olive or peanut oil for the pan

Hushpuppies, to serve

Lemon wedges, to serve

1. **MAKE THE TARTAR SAUCE.** Whisk the mayonnaise, relish, horseradish, mustard, lemon juice, and hot sauce in a small bowl until fully combined. Store in a lidded container in the refrigerator until serving time and use within 2 to 3 weeks.

2. Mix the medium- and fine-grind cornmeal in a shallow dish with the garlic, salt, and several grinds of pepper.

3. Whisk the eggs with the hot sauce in a medium mixing bowl.

4. One by one, coat the catfish fillets in the egg mixture, then lightly dredge them in the cornmeal mixture. Set aside on a large plate or platter.

5. Lightly coat the bottom of a cast iron skillet with oil and warm over medium heat. Add the catfish fillets and cook in batches, about 2 to 3 minutes per side, depending on thickness. Add oil to the pan between batches when necessary, to prevent sticking. Serve immediately with tartar sauce, hushpuppies, and lemon wedges.

POTATO CHIPS

The southern United States cannot lay claim to the potato chip's provenance. While a variety of competing theories exist, none of them situate the point of origin in the Southern states. One popular legend posits that potato chips as we know them today owe to the efforts of one George Crum. A chef at Moon's Lake House in Saratoga Springs, New York, Crum was attempting to placate an unhappy customer who kept sending his French-fried potatoes back to the kitchen, claiming they had been cut too thick.

The mythology maintains Crum cut the potatoes extremely thin, fried them in oil until crisp, and seasoned them with salt. All of which apparently resulted in a very happy customer, who was later claimed to be none other than Cornelius Vanderbilt. Accordingly, the chips went on to be referred to as "Saratoga chips," and were called by this name until sometime in the twentieth century.

So, though they may not be inherently capital S "Southern," potato chips were decidedly an integral part of my Southern childhood, and were always on offer at the restaurants we patronized and the homes we visited. It's for these reasons that I opted to include them as a necessary component of a Southern kitchen. Growing up, mom always had potato chips in the house. Personally, I don't think this is necessarily the best idea, as where there are chips, there are mouths looking to mindlessly snack on them. I am nearly always appalled by the amount of chips I can eat out of a bag without realizing it. Homemade chips are therefore a great solution. You satisfy that delicious salty, crunchy hankering, but in a quantity that's far more manageable. I think mom, George Crum, and even Cornelius Vanderbilt would approve.

SERVING SUGGESTIONS
- *Crumble atop a green bean casserole for a crunchy, salty contrast.*
- *Serve with Sour Cream Bacon Dip (page 209) and experience Southern snack nirvana.*
- *Enjoy with a Rosemary Apple Shrub (page 91) for a salty foil to the tangy beverage.*
- *Pair with a Southern Reuben (page 118).*

POTATO CHIPS
· SERVES 2 TO 4 ·

1½ pounds russet potatoes (skins on)

½ cup white vinegar

Peanut or light olive oil

Sea salt

1. Thinly slice the potatoes (preferably with a mandoline) between ¹⁄₁₆ and ⅛ inch.

2. Rinse the potatoes with cool water and place in a medium bowl. Cover the potatoes with ice water and the white vinegar. Leave to rest for 30 minutes.

3. Toward the final 10 minutes of resting time, preheat the oven to 400°F. Place a wire cooling rack atop a large rimmed baking sheet.

4. Heat 2 inches of oil to 350°F in a large pot or Dutch oven. Hold the temperature steady.

5. Remove the potatoes from the ice water bath. Place them in a single layer on a kitchen cloth and pat to dry. Evenly lay the slices across the wire cooling rack. Bake the chips in batches for 5 minutes. Remove the pan from the oven.

6. In small batches, one layer deep at a time, add the chips to the hot oil one by one so that they don't stick. Cook the chips for about 6 minutes, until the bubbling starts to slow down and they turn golden brown.

7. With a kitchen spider or slotted spoon, remove the chips to a bowl lined with paper towels.

8. Gently toss the chips with salt, to taste.

9. Bring the temperature of the oil back up to 350°F. Repeat the process until all of the potatoes have been fried in the oil.

10. Serve the chips immediately, or store in an airtight lidded container or resealable bag and consume within 2 to 3 days.

MAC & CHEESE WITH POTATO CHIP CRUST

· SERVES 6 TO 8 ·

The crispy potato crust makes this dish even more delicious than you ever thought possible. Serve this to children and witness a meal without the need for coaxing or bribery. This is comfort food for any age at its finest.

---

1 pound gobetti pasta, or similar short
    noodle pasta

2 tablespoons extra-virgin olive oil

1 medium onion, diced

2 garlic cloves, minced

3 tablespoons Butter (page 194)

3 tablespoons all-purpose flour

2 cups whole milk, warmed slightly

20 ounces cheddar cheese, grated

½ teaspoon grated nutmeg

1 teaspoon hot sauce

Sea salt and freshly ground pepper

4 large eggs, beaten

1 cup crushed Potato Chips

1. Cook the pasta to al dente, according to the package instructions. Liberally butter a 9 x 13-inch casserole dish. Set aside. Preheat the oven to 350°F.

2. Warm the olive oil over medium heat in a large saucepan. Add the onion and sauté for about 8 minutes, until browned slightly and fragrant. Add the minced garlic, and sauté for a couple minutes longer. Transfer to a bowl and set aside.

3. Return the pan to the stovetop and melt the butter over medium heat. Add the flour and stir for about 1 minute, creating a roux, until blond and smooth.

4. Little by little, whisk in the warmed milk. Continue to whisk the roux for another 1 to 2 minutes, until smooth and starting to bubble.

5. Add 16 ounces of the cheese and stir until melted and smooth. Stir in the onion mixture, nutmeg, hot sauce, a pinch of salt, and several grinds of pepper.

6. Remove the cheese sauce from the heat, and stir in the eggs until fully combined.

7. Combine the cooked pasta and the cheese sauce in the prepared casserole dish until the noodles are evenly coated with sauce. Top with the remaining 4 ounces of grated cheese.

8. In a small mixing bowl, combine the crushed potato chips with a pinch of salt and a few grinds of pepper. Top the casserole evenly with the potato chips.

9. Bake for 40 to 45 minutes, until bubbly and golden on top. If desired, carefully broil for a minute if you'd like a browner top. Let cool for 15 minutes before serving.

SOUTHERN-SEASONED POTATO CHIPS

· SERVES 2 TO 4 ·

If you want to give your chips a little extra something, sprinkle this seasoning on them. Adjust the saltiness and heat according to your liking. This recipe will make more Cajun Seasoning than you will need. Store the remainder in a lidded container and use it with Boiled Peanuts (page 164), add to Southern Greens (page 20), or sprinkle anywhere you feel food could use a kick of flavor and heat.

FOR THE CAJUN SEASONING
¼ cup sea salt
¼ cup smoked paprika
2 tablespoons granulated garlic
2 tablespoons ground sumac
2 tablespoons onion granules

1 tablespoon ground black pepper
1 tablespoon ground cayenne
1 teaspoon chipotle powder

OTHER INGREDIENTS
1 batch Potato Chips

1. Make the Cajun seasoning. Combine the salt, paprika, garlic, sumac, onion, pepper, cayenne, and chipotle powder in a small bowl and stir to fully blend. Store at room temperature out of direct sunlight in a lidded airtight container. Use within 6 months.

2. Prepare potato chips as directed on page 157.

3. As soon as each batch of chips comes out of the fryer, sprinkle them with 2 to 3 teaspoons of the seasoning. Serve immediately.

NUTS

A wide variety of nuts, both wild and cultivated, have been an integral part of Southern cuisine for centuries. From acorns to hickory nuts, chestnuts to beechnuts, pecans to black walnuts, Native Americans were gathering and baking assorted dishes with wild nuts when the colonists arrived. Nuts were rendered into cooking oils, butters, flours, and more. Those products then became the foundation of cakes, puddings, cookies, milks, teas, medicines, and more, as well as being used as dye matter for natural coloring.

Pecans, native to Mexico and the Southern states, didn't become widely cultivated until late in the nineteenth century. They are now grown in such abundance domestically that the United States accounts for the largest global percentage of pecan cultivation. English walnuts came to the United States later, after being introduced into Europe from Persia. Colonists and explorers crossing the Atlantic brought these revered nuts to the New World.

The nuts of my upbringing were pretty much limited to pecans, peanuts (not a true nut, but we'll let it slide), and walnuts. No pine nuts or fancy pistachios in Mom's pantry, thank you kindly. That came later, when we moved to Black Mountain, North Carolina, during my sophomore year of high school, and I became practically bewitched by the multitudinous nut offerings at the nearby French Broad Food Co-op. Those pecans, peanuts, and walnuts consumed with frequency in my youth have become the nuts I most prefer now, as an adult. If you're so inclined, and have access to them, here is how to dry and store fresh nuts.

SERVING SUGGESTIONS

- *Enjoy a handful of Boiled Peanuts (page 164) with a hard cider. The crisp sweetness of the cider is an excellent contrast to the salt and spice of the peanuts.*
- *Sprinkle black walnuts over a salad of Bibb lettuce and clementine segments, and drizzle with Apple Butter Vinaigrette (page 62).*
- *Spread Pecan Coins (page 165) with Pimento Cheese (page 33) and Pickled Okra rounds (page 27).*

NUTS

· AMOUNT VARIES ·

Peanuts, pecans, or black walnuts

FOR PEANUTS

1. Once the leaves on the plant begin to yellow in autumn, it's time to check the pods for harvest. If the pods are nearly full, loosen up the soil around the plant, pull out the plant, shake off the soil, and hang the plants in a warm, dry location for 3 weeks.
2. Remove the pods from the plant, and compost the plant and roots. Spread out the pods in a single layer on a flat surface and keep in a warm, dry area for 2 weeks. Store in a mesh bag, such as those used for purchasing produce. Keep out of direct sunlight and away from moisture. Use within 3 to 4 months.

FOR PECANS AND BLACK WALNUTS

1. Both pecans and black walnuts, like peanuts, are ready for harvest in autumn. When their green hulls open or simply drop from the tree, it's time to harvest the nuts. Collect as soon as possible to avoid mold.

2. Pecans will come right out of their hulls, but some black walnuts may still be in theirs. To remove, you can purchase a de-huller or spread out the walnuts on a tarp, cover them, and drive over them. Once free of their hulls, rinse the walnuts to remove any debris.

3. Both types of nuts need to be dried in the shell. Spread them out in an even layer on a flat surface or drying screen. Set outside on a warm day to air dry. Pecans need to dry for 2 weeks, while black walnuts need 3 to 4 days of hot, dry airing.

4. Test for doneness by removing a bit of the nut meat from the shell. If it seems brittle and snaps easily when broken in half, the nuts are dried and can be stored.

5. Store in-shell pecans at room temperature in an airtight lidded container, and use within 6 months. Store shelled pecans in a freezer bag or airtight container in the refrigerator or freezer and use within 6 months to 1 year. Store in-shell or shelled black walnuts in a freezer bag or airtight container in the freezer and use within 6 months to 1 year. You may also store shelled pecans or black walnuts in an airtight container at room temperature, but they will need to be used within 1 to 2 months.

BOILED PEANUTS

· MAKES 1½ POUNDS ·

Raw peanuts can be difficult to source. Unless you grow your own, have a nearby farmer that does, or are inclined to order them by mail, you'll most likely be working with dried raw peanuts. Either fresh or dried will produce equally tasty boiled nuts; dried peanuts simply require some soaking time, as indicated in this recipe.

1½ pounds raw green or dried raw peanuts

⅔ cup sea salt

10 cups water

3 tablespoons Cajun seasoning (page 160)

1. If using dried raw peanuts, place in a large bowl. Cover with cold water and leave to soak for 8 to 12 hours. Otherwise, rinse the peanuts in cold water, drain, and place in a slow cooker.
2. Add the salt, water, and Cajun seasoning. Stir with a wooden spoon to combine the spices with the water.
3. Put the lid on the slow cooker and cook on low for 20 to 24 hours, until the peanuts are fully softened.
4. Drain off the cooking liquid and serve immediately. They can also be stored in a lidded container in the refrigerator and consumed within 2 to 3 days.

CANDIED BLACK WALNUTS

· MAKES ABOUT 1 CUP ·

Black walnuts have a deeply distinct flavor. Lacking the characteristic sweetness of their English cousins, black walnuts possess a taste best described as resinous or earthy. I love them, particularly when they are candied. Whether served with a dessert or as a midday snack, these nuts are sure to delight.

¼ cup sugar

1 cup black walnuts, lightly toasted

1. Line a large rimmed baking sheet with parchment paper or a silicone baking mat.
2. Put the sugar in a heavy-bottomed saucepan and add just enough water to create a texture and consistency resembling wet sand.
3. Warm the pan over medium-high heat until the sugar has melted and is fully liquefied.
4. Remove the pan from the heat, stir in the walnuts until fully coated by the sugar syrup, and then spread them out evenly on the baking sheet.
5. Leave the walnuts to cool for 15 minutes, and then break apart into individual pieces, as needed. Store at room temperature in an airtight, lidded container. Use within 1 month.

PECAN COINS

· MAKES ABOUT 3 DOZEN ·

These crackers are about as iconic of a Southern cracker as you can find. Buttery and robust, they hold up well to whatever you spread on them.

8 ounces sharp cheddar cheese, grated

6 tablespoons Butter, room temperature (page 194)

1 cup all-purpose flour

½ teaspoon sea salt

¼ teaspoon ground cayenne

¼ teaspoon ground coriander

¼ teaspoon ground cumin

¼ teaspoon granulated garlic

½ cup toasted pecans, finely chopped

1. Place the cheese and butter in a food processor or mixer. Mix until fully combined.

2. Add the flour, salt, cayenne, coriander, cumin, and garlic. Mix until the dough begins to form a ball.

3. Add the pecans and mix just until the nuts are evenly distributed throughout the dough.

4. Divide the dough into three portions. Place one portion on a sheet of parchment or wax paper. Shape it into a log about 1¼ inches round and roll it up in the paper. Twist each of the ends, securing the dough.

5. Repeat with the two other portions of dough. Place the three logs in the refrigerator and chill for 2 to 3 hours.

6. Preheat the oven to 350°F. Line two large rimmed baking pans with parchment paper or silicone baking mats.

7. Slice each log into 12 coins and place on the prepared pans. Bake for 20 to 22 minutes, rotating the pans halfway through the baking time, until the coins begin to brown on the edges.

8. Remove the pans from the oven. Cool in the pan for 5 minutes, and then transfer to wire cooling racks. Store at room temperature in airtight lidded containers. Use within 5 to 7 days.

BEANS

Southerners are huge fans of beans. From pots of slow-cooked green beans, simmered for several hours with a piece of country ham or some bacon drippings until limp and fragrant, to black-eyed peas, brought to the New World by African slaves, beans have been part of the Southern landscape forever. Native Americans revered beans so greatly that they placed them second only to corn in their regard.

Beans have undergone extensive cultivation, hybridization, and experimentation in the New World. In the Southern states, pole beans, string beans, green beans, red beans, black beans, lima beans, butter beans, black-eyed peas, crowder peas, and navy beans are but a small sampling of the most commonly grown varieties. European and Asian varieties have been introduced as well, so it's now possible to maintain a Southern garden with a veritable Union Nation's worth of beans.

The culinary foundation of cultures the world over, beans are economical and nutrient powerhouses, which most likely explains their global appeal. The beans I grew up with are those I list here. If you find yourself in possession of fresh beans, either because you grew them, you bought them, or someone gave them to you, here's how to dry and store them for later use.

SERVING SUGGESTIONS

- *Beans are highly versatile and have infinite uses. Render into all manner of soups and hearty stews.*
- *Use navy beans in making baked beans.*
- *Slow cook lima beans with a bit of bacon grease to infuse their subtle flavor with a hint of smokiness.*

BEANS

· AMOUNT VARIES ·

Navy, kidney, butter, great northern,
 pinto, and lima beans, and field peas

1. Leave the bean pods on the vine until you can hear them rattling inside when shaken. Only when the pods and vines are thoroughly dry and shriveled up should you harvest the pods.
2. Shell the beans by removing them from their pods. Compost or discard the pods. If the beans still feel moist, use a food dehydrator or set on drying racks in the sun over the course of several warm, sunny days, bringing in the trays at night, until the beans feel fully dry and are glossy.
3. In order to kill insects and their eggs, spread out the dried beans across a large rimmed baking pan. Place in an oven set to its lowest setting, and warm for 30 minutes. Cool, and then store the beans in an airtight, lidded container at room temperature out of direct sunlight.

SOUTHERN-STYLE PINTO BEANS

· SERVES 6 TO 8 ·

A soupy pot of pinto beans was one of my step-grandfather Papa John's most beloved foods. He'd ladle out a bowl, cover it liberally with chopped onions, cut a wedge of cornbread out of the skillet, crumble it over the top, and dig in with contentment. May we all be so easily satisfied.

1 pound dry pinto beans

1 medium onion, peeled and halved

4 slices pork fatback

1 teaspoon smoked paprika

1 Dried Pepper (page 124)

Sea salt and freshly ground black pepper

1. Rinse the pinto beans in a colander with cold water. Place the beans in a medium bowl, cover with cold water, at least 4 inches above the beans, and leave to soak for 8 to 12 hours at room temperature.
2. Rinse the beans again in a colander, rinsing and stirring until the water runs clear.
3. Fill a large pot or Dutch oven halfway with cold water. Add the beans, onion, fatback, paprika, and dried pepper, and bring to a boil over medium-high heat.
4. Reduce the heat to low, cover the pot with a lid, and simmer for 1 to 2 hours, stirring occasionally. Monitor the liquid level and adjust as needed, making sure that the beans remain covered by at least 1 inch of liquid at all times.
5. When the beans are tender, add salt and pepper to taste. Serve immediately.

HOPPIN' JOHN

· SERVES 6 TO 8 ·

For my entire life nearly without fail, I have eaten Hoppin' John every New Year's day, even during those years I kept a vegan or vegetarian diet. I think it's safe to call consuming it a Southern New Year's ritual. A dish of black-eyed peas and rice, served alongside collard greens, the meal is believed to be auspicious, bringing luck and fortune in the year to come, with the beans representing coins and the greens paper currency. It's far too delicious, however, to eat only once a year.

2 cups black-eyed peas or cowpeas

1 tablespoon Bacon Drippings (page 176)

1 celery stalk, diced

1 medium yellow onion, chopped

1 red bell pepper, chopped

2 garlic cloves, minced

4 cups Chicken Stock (page 187)

1 teaspoon dried thyme

1 teaspoon sea salt

2 bay leaves

1 ham hock

Freshly ground black pepper

Several dashes of hot sauce

2 cups cooked white rice

Southern Greens (page 20), to serve

1. Put the black-eyed peas in a medium mixing bowl, cover with hot tap water, and leave to soak for 2 hours. Drain off the soaking water and set the peas aside.

2. Warm the bacon drippings over medium heat in a large pot or Dutch oven. Add the celery, onion, and bell pepper, and sauté for 8 to 10 minutes, until the vegetables are fragrant and limp.

3. Add the garlic and sauté for 1 minute. Add the soaked peas, stock, thyme, salt, bay leaves, ham hock, and several grinds of pepper. Reduce the heat to low and simmer for 30 to 35 minutes, until the peas are tender but not mushy.

4. Drain the peas and place them in a medium mixing bowl. Check the salt, adjusting to taste as needed.

5. Remove the ham hock, and use a fork to pull the ham off the bone. Cut any large pieces into smaller ones, and add back to the bowl of peas. Stir in the hot sauce, rice, and Southern Greens. Serve immediately.

6

FATS
— & —
MEATS

LARD

—————

For centuries, the vast availability of wild game and fish provided all the animal protein that Native Americans and colonists needed to survive. From passenger pigeons to wild turkeys, deer to buffalo, and all manner of creatures in between, the demand for domesticated animals for food needs was slim. Over time, food sources diminished as the human population increased, and other animals became both needed and desired.

The animal stepping in to meet that need, and maintaining prime status until the 1900s, was the pig. They are relatively easy to maintain, inexpensive to feed, and increase their bodily mass very expediently. In contrast to cows, which require large amounts of grazing land, pigs require a modicum of space and are happy to eat whatever they're presented with. They are also nearly entirely edible, so there's very little waste when processing hogs versus other animals. Though beef has supplanted pork as the most widely consumed U.S. animal protein, it's still king in the Southern states.

Technically speaking, lard is fat from a pig. The term lard refers to both rendered (cooked) and unrendered (raw) forms of the fat. Rendering lard helps make it shelf-stable and removes any impurities or components other than the fat itself. Fat from a pig comes from its back, belly, and around its kidneys. This last type of pig fat, referred to as "leaf lard," is thought to be the cleanest fat on the pig, yielding the most white, odorless rendered lard, highly versatile in all forms of cooking and baking, from frying and roasting to forming into pie crusts.

SERVING SUGGESTIONS

- *Substitute lard for the butter in Pie Dough (page 217) to impart abundant flakiness.*
- *Lard can handle high heat quite well. Use when tempura frying vegetables (you'll need a pretty good amount of lard in order to do this).*
- *You might balk at first, but trust me on this one. Lard is delicious spread on bread and eaten straight, just like butter.*
- *Warm a bit of lard and toss with cubed red potatoes; roast at 400°F until crispy and golden, 15 to 20 minutes.*

—————

LARD

· MAKES ABOUT 1 QUART ·

—————

3 pounds leaf lard, frozen

1. Cut the leaf lard into roughly 1-inch chunks.
2. Transfer the fat to a slow cooker. Cover with a lid and set to low.
3. After a few hours, give the fat a stir. Once liquid begins to cover any remaining unmelted portion, remove the lid.

4. Let the lard continue to heat on low, stirring occasionally, for 6 to 8 hours, until the solid fat mass has fully liquefied.

5. Line a funnel with fine-mesh cheesecloth or butter muslin and secure it in place with a rubber band. Rest the funnel on a quart Mason jar. Using a ladle, begin to pour the liquid into the funnel. If any solid bits remain behind ("cracklins"), use them to flavor foods or give to your pets. The longer the lard cooks, the more of a pork or pig flavor it will have. It will also change in color from white to off-white. If you want a more neutral-flavored lard for using in biscuits and sweet fruit pies, strain off the first ladlefuls into smaller jars.

6. Store the lard in the refrigerator and use within 6 months.

PIGGY POPCORN

· MAKES ABOUT 6 CUPS ·

Popcorn made with pig components will put your other popcorn to shame. Cooked in lard and then punctuated throughout with bacon, this popcorn satisfies your crunchy, salty, smoky cravings all in the same bite.

½ pound Bacon (page 176)
2 tablespoons Lard

½ cup popcorn
Sea salt

1. Cook the bacon until crispy, either on the stovetop for about 7 to 9 minutes or in the oven (as per page 64). Remove the cooked strips to a plate lined with a paper towel. Once cooled, crumble into large pieces.

2. Place the lard in a large pot, an enamel-coated Dutch oven, or an electric popcorn maker. Warm the pot over medium heat and add the popcorn once the lard has melted (or proceed according to the popcorn maker's instructions).

3. Cover the pot and give it a little shake to coat the kernels with lard. Listen for popping to begin, and then for it to slow. Once it slows but doesn't fully stop, remove from the heat.

4. Transfer the popcorn to a large bowl, and toss in the bacon pieces. Add salt to taste and serve immediately.

SWEET POTATO FRENCH FRIES

· SERVES 4 ·

Many people aren't aware of the delicious transformation that happens to vegetables roasted in lard. They crisp up perfectly and brown evenly. These fries won't necessarily have the same snap and crunch of deep-fried potatoes, but they do have a glorious mouthfeel and flavor.

2 medium sweet potatoes

2 tablespoons Lard

2 teaspoons coarse salt

1 teaspoon smoked paprika

1. Preheat the oven to 450°F. Cut the sweet potatoes into French fry–size thickness and length, leaving the skin on.
2. Place the lard on a large rimmed baking sheet. Put the sheet in the oven and monitor the lard. As soon as it has melted, remove the sheet from the oven.
3. Add the potatoes to the pan, carefully tossing them with the lard, until each piece is well coated. Spread out the potatoes in a single layer, taking care that the pieces don't overlap.
4. Sprinkle the potatoes evenly with 1 teaspoon of the salt and ½ teaspoon of the paprika. Place the sheet in the oven and bake for 15 minutes.
5. Remove the sheet from the oven, and using either kitchen tongs or your fingers, flip each fry over. Sprinkle with the remaining 1 teaspoon salt and ½ teaspoon paprika, and put the sheet back in the oven for 20 minutes, until browned and crispy. Serve immediately.

BACON & DRIPPINGS

Oh, bacon. So delicious, so beloved, so capable of causing vegetarians to lapse. Bacon is in a class by itself. Every bite is revelry. It is perfection on its own and it makes almost any dish better. Someone who says they love you more than bacon is probably lying—but if not, their love is vast.

Come butchering time, hogs can easily weigh several hundred pounds. Their abundant size equates to large quantities of meat and meat products requiring immediate preservation. Before the advent of refrigeration and freezing, clever means of preserving hogs without electricity were employed, including drying, salting, and smoking.

The word "bacon" has French and German origins, and originally meant the back of a pig. The term as it is used today, however, developed in sixteenth-century England, refers to pork that has undergone smoking and salting. That said, records dating as far back as 1500 B.C.E. refer to bacon, when the ancient Chinese preserved pork by means of salting. Documents in ancient Rome also point to an early variation of bacon.

I loved when my grandmother Nanny would talk about hog butchering time with her family in Henry County, Virginia. Her parents, my great-grandparents Mamaw and Papaw, would gather with other neighboring families each autumn to collectively butcher and process a hog or two that they had raised. It was a community affair, with the men doing the butchering and the women doing the preserving. I often think of my extended family whenever I enjoy a crispy strip of bacon or cut into a pork chop. This recipe for homemade bacon generously comes from my friend Jeremiah DeBrie of the Asheville, North Carolina–based sustainable butchery Intentional Swine. From terrines to bacon, he knows his way around swine like the best of them.

SERVING SUGGESTIONS

- *Serve bacon over a blend of lettuces with an over easy egg for a breakfast salad packed with smoke, salt, creaminess, and earthiness. Roasted tomatoes and crispy potatoes will round out the dish even further.*
- *Crumble bacon over Vanilla Ice Cream (page 210) for a sweet, salty treat.*
- *Warm a tablespoon of drippings over medium heat in a pan, and then use it to fry hot dogs. Sprinkle with a bit of smoky paprika and serve in buns with spicy mustard and Sweet Pickle Relish (page 30).*

BACON & DRIPPINGS
· MAKES 6 TO 7 POUNDS ·

---

1 side pork belly, about 10 pounds, skin on
   or off
¼ to ½ cup bourbon

Dry cure mix: 1 pound salt, 8 ounces sweetener
   (molasses, honey, or brown sugar), and
   1 ounce #1 curing salts (pink salt optional)
Freshly ground black pepper

FOR THE BACON

1. Trim the pork belly into a shape and size that is compatible with whatever nonreactive storage container and/or smoking unit you intend to use.

2. Rub the belly with bourbon. Next, season with 3 ounces of dry cure to every 5 pounds of meat. Place in a nonreactive container, cover, and refrigerate for 5 days (7 days if the belly is particularly thick). Flip the meat over daily and massage it in the natural brine.

3. After 5 days, remove the pork belly from the container, rinse it, and rub the flesh side with pepper.

4. Prepare your smoker to 250°F. Smoke the belly to reach an internal temperature of 155°F. If the skin is still attached, it's easiest to peel it off while still hot (save the skin to add to soups or stocks).

5. Let cool for at least 8 hours in the refrigerator, and then store tightly wrapped. Use within 7 to 10 days. Alternatively, store in a resealable bag or lidded container in the freezer and use within 6 weeks.

6. When ready to use, the bacon can be cooked in a large pot or Dutch oven over medium heat until it starts to get crispy, about 7 to 9 minutes, then allow it to drain on a paper towel. Alternatively, bake the bacon in a preheated 400°F oven. Place a cooling rack over a large rimmed baking sheet and arrange the bacon slices on the cooling rack. Bake for 15 to 20 minutes, until browned and fragrant.

FOR THE DRIPPINGS

1. When the bacon is done, remove it from the pan, and pour the drippings into a heatproof container.

2. Cover with a lid, and store at room temperature out of direct sunlight. Use within 3 to 4 months.

BOURBON BACON JAM

· MAKES ABOUT 2 CUPS ·

This jam is *the* jam. Which is to say that it is pretty much sublime, if you like bacon, bourbon, and, well, deliciousness in general. We like it simply spread on a cracker, but it would work equally well on a fried egg sandwich or smeared onto a steak.

---

1 pound Bacon, cut into thick strips	½ cup bourbon
2 tablespoons Bacon Drippings	½ cup light brown sugar
1 large onion, diced	2 tablespoons sorghum syrup
¼ cup water	1 tablespoon lemon juice

1. Preheat the oven to 400°F. Lay the bacon strips atop wire cooling racks placed on two large rimmed baking sheets (or on one baking sheet in batches). Bake for 15 minutes and then turn the strips over. Bake for 5 to 10 minutes longer, until the bacon starts to get just a little crispy around the edges. Remove the pan(s) from the oven and set aside to cool.

2. Warm a medium saucepan over medium heat. Add the bacon drippings. Once melted, add the onion. Sauté for 15 minutes, until nicely browned around the edges.

3. While the onions cook, chop the bacon into small pieces.

4. Add the water, bourbon, brown sugar, sorghum, and lemon juice to the pan, stirring to fully combine. Cook for about 10 minutes, until syrupy, and then add the bacon. Cook for 5 minutes longer, stirring frequently, then remove from the heat.

5. Serve immediately, or store in the refrigerator and consume within 7 to 10 days.

SAVORY BACON, LEEK & MUSHROOM BREAD PUDDING

· SERVES 6 TO 8 ·

Savory bread puddings are a crowd pleaser. They yield a large portion, perfect for holidays, weekend brunches, baby showers, or anytime a generous breakfast/lunch entrée is desired.

---

6 strips Bacon

3 large leeks, cleaned, cut into ½-inch strips, and coarsely chopped

1 pound wild mushrooms or mushroom of your choice, coarsely chopped

2 cups heavy cream

2 cups whole milk

1 tablespoon Worcestershire sauce

1 tablespoon dried thyme

1 tablespoon dried tarragon

2 teaspoons sea salt

6 eggs, beaten

1 loaf crusty white bread (about 1½ pounds), cubed

1 cup loosely packed, grated smoked Gouda cheese

1. Warm a large pot or Dutch oven over medium heat. Put the bacon in the pot, and cook just until it starts to get crispy. Remove the cooked strips to a plate lined with a paper towel. Once cooled, crumble the bacon into large pieces.

2. Add the leeks and mushrooms to the bacon grease in the pot. Sauté for 10 minutes, until wilted and fragrant. Stir in the cream, milk, Worcestershire sauce, thyme, tarragon, and salt, and gently simmer for 15 minutes. Remove from the heat.

3. Stir in the eggs until fully incorporated. Fold in the bread and bacon, cover the pot loosely with a kitchen cloth, and let sit at room temperature for 1 hour, occasionally stirring gently.

4. During the last 10 minutes of resting time, preheat the oven to 375°F. Liberally butter a 9 x 13-inch pan. Pour the filling into the pan and top with the cheese. Bake for 1 hour, until the pudding has set and the cheese is golden brown. Let cool for at least 20 minutes before serving.

SUCCOTASH

· SERVES 6 TO 8 ·

In the summer of 2016, I stopped by my friend Elliott Moss's Asheville, North Carolina, whole hog restaurant, Buxton Hall, for lunch. As he often generously does whenever he happens to see us from the kitchen, Elliott brought us out a sample of something he'd been working on. On this particular occasion, that happened to be succotash.

Mind you, I grew up eating succotash, a dish containing lima beans, sweet corn, other field beans, and sometimes okra and tomatoes. Elliott's succotash, however, was both familiar and brand new. In short, it was the best, most enlivening iteration of succotash that I had ever tasted, and serves as the inspiration for my version here. Though different, our dishes share the same brightness and freshness, infusing each bite with the essence of summertime.

---

3 strips Bacon

1 onion, diced

1 red bell pepper, diced

½ pound okra, cut into bite-size rounds

3 garlic cloves, minced

1 pound yellow summer squash, roughly chopped

½ cup Butter (page 194)

½ pound cherry tomatoes, halved if small, quartered if large

5 ears corn, shucked and cut from the cob (about 2½ cups)

1 pound baby lima beans, cooked to al dente

2 teaspoons sea salt

Freshly ground black pepper

1 cup chopped fresh basil leaves

1. Warm a Dutch oven or large pot over medium heat. Place the bacon into the pan and cook just until it starts to get crispy. Remove the cooked strips to a plate lined with a paper towel. Once cooled, crumble or chop the bacon into small pieces.

2. Add the onion, bell pepper, and okra to the bacon grease in the pot. Sauté for 10 to 12 minutes, until the vegetables begin to brown around the edges.

3. Stir in the garlic and cook for 1 minute. Stir in the squash and cook for 5 minutes. Stir in the reserved bacon pieces. Add the butter, stirring until melted.

4. Stir in the cherry tomatoes, corn, lima beans, salt, and several grinds of pepper. Reduce the heat to low and simmer for 20 minutes, stirring occasionally.

5. Remove the pot from the heat and stir in the basil. Let sit for a few minutes, and stir before serving.

BREAKFAST SAUSAGE

Some might call my Southern credentials into question over what I'm about to say, but it's true—I'd take breakfast sausage over bacon any day. Heresy, I know, especially given how much I truly do love bacon. But I simply cannot get enough of breakfast sausage's mix of herbs, spices, and fat. It satisfies seemingly all of my flavor cravings.

Though available today throughout the United States, breakfast, or country, sausage is most often associated with the South, especially its more rural areas. Farmers, wanting to make as large a return on their commodities as possible, would often grind up any remaining scraps and parts of hogs after processing. The resulting ground pork was then combined with herbs and spices, and either fried as patties or encased in tubing, and enjoyed by the farmer himself and his farm crew. Hence, the "country" reference in country sausage.

Breakfast sausage is something that I have never not known. Which is to say, a package of it was always in our refrigerator or enjoyed with biscuits and gravy when dining out. Here's my take on the breakfast sausage I grew up with, which we'd purchase packed in a wide plastic tube, ends twisted over with metal clamps.

SERVING SUGGESTIONS

- *Sausage and tomatoes complement each other nicely, the fat of the meat tempering the tartness of the fruits. Brown and stir into a tomato sauce as a hearty, fragrant topping for pasta.*
- *Brown and crumble, then use as a taco filling. Top with Sour Cream (page 207), grated cheddar, radish slices, salsa, and chopped cilantro.*
- *Fry patties and sandwich between Buttermilk Biscuits (page 147) for an at-the-ready meal.*

BREAKFAST SAUSAGE

· MAKES 1 POUND ·

---

1 pound ground pork	½ teaspoon dried thyme
1 tablespoon dried rubbed sage	½ teaspoon fennel seeds, crushed
1½ teaspoons sea salt	¼ teaspoon red pepper flakes
½ teaspoon granulated garlic	¼ teaspoon ground nutmeg
½ teaspoon freshly ground black pepper	¼ teaspoon ground coriander

1. Put the pork, sage, salt, garlic, black pepper, thyme, fennel seeds, pepper flakes, nutmeg, and coriander in a bowl.
2. Using clean hands, squish the meat into the seasonings until fully combined.
3. Place a large sheet of parchment or wax paper on the counter. Transfer the meat to the paper, and form into a log about 6 to 8 inches long.
4. Store in the refrigerator and use within 5 days, or transfer the roll (still in the paper) to a sealable freezer bag or container, store in the freezer, and use within 3 to 4 months.

SAUSAGE MEATBALLS
WITH HOT PEPPER JELLY GLAZE

· MAKES ABOUT 4 DOZEN ·

If you're having a party, make these meatballs. I don't care if you're entertaining an all-women, all-men, or mixed crowd, the meatballs will be equally met with praise and adulation. Just remember to grab a few for yourself before the guests arrive, otherwise you'll blink and the platter will be empty.

2 eggs, beaten

¼ cup Buttermilk (page 199)

Hot sauce (optional)

2 pounds Breakfast Sausage

2 cups Cornbread crumbs (page 142, see Note)

1 half-pint (1 cup) Hot Pepper Jelly (page 82)

Olive oil

NOTE: Place cornbread in a food processor and quickly pulse just until fine crumbs form.

1. Place a wire cooling rack atop a large rimmed baking sheet and set aside.
2. Whisk the eggs with the buttermilk in a large bowl. If you want the meatballs on the spicy side, add a few shakes of hot sauce.
3. Add the sausage and cornbread crumbs to the egg mixture. Using clean hands, knead the ingredients together until fully combined. Set aside to rest for 5 minutes.
4. Roll the mixture into rounds about the size of ping-pong balls.
5. Warm ¼ inch of olive oil in a saucepan over medium-low heat. Cook the meatballs in batches, turning them frequently, for about 10 minutes, until nicely browned and cooked through.
6. Transfer the meatballs to the cooling rack to drain.
7. While the meatballs cool, warm the pepper jelly in a small pan over medium heat until it becomes fully liquefied and syrupy.
8. Transfer the meatballs to a large bowl and pour the pepper jelly syrup over them. Using a large spoon, gently toss the meatballs in the syrup.
9. Serve immediately, or set aside and gently warm on a baking sheet when you are ready to serve.

SAUSAGE GRAVY WITH BUTTERMILK BISCUITS

· SERVES 4 ·

Biscuits and gravy. Those three words alone cause my shoulders to relax and my breath to steady. I love that combination of foods the way Elvis loved his mama, unabashedly and for all to know. I sincerely hope that this recipe produces the same joy in you and your loved ones as it does for me and mine.

1 pound Breakfast Sausage

5 tablespoons all-purpose flour

4 tablespoons Butter, room temperature (page 194)

3 cups whole milk, room temperature or slightly warmed

Sea salt and freshly ground black pepper

Buttermilk Biscuits, warmed (page 147)

1. Warm a medium saucepan over medium-high heat. Add the sausage and cook for 8 minutes, until cooked through and lightly browned.

2. Scoop out the sausage into a fine-mesh sieve set atop a heatproof jar. Drain off any excess fat. If any fat remains in the pan, remove all but 1 tablespoon. Reduce the heat to low.

3. Add the flour and butter to the pan, stirring with a large spoon until the mixture is completely smooth. Over low heat, cook until the roux is melted and light golden in color.

4. Pour in a small splash of the milk, and stir to incorporate. Continue adding a splash at a time, stirring after each addition until fully combined.

5. Once all the milk is incorporated, add a pinch of salt, a few grinds of pepper, and the sausage. Gently simmer for 10 to 12 minutes, stirring frequently, until the gravy is a little thinner than you want it to be (it will thicken as it cools). Remove the pan from the heat. Serve immediately with warm biscuits.

STOCK (PORK, CHICKEN & BEEF)

While it is true that making your own stock takes a bit of time, most of it is hands-free, setting a timer and walking away as the liquid simmers and reduces. Technically speaking, stocks are composed of flavor-forward vegetables (often onions or leeks, carrots, celery, and, sometimes, garlic), aromatic herbs and spices, and meat, fish, or additional vegetables as the main flavoring components. To that medley, you add water along with a wide range of other potential ingredients, such as wine, Worcestershire sauce, tomato paste, soy sauce, salt, and more.

How does broth differ from stock? When making stock, you strain all the ingredients through a fine-mesh sieve, leaving only the liquid behind for use. With broths, bits of the ingredients often remain in the finished dish. It took me a long time to remember the difference between the two (longer than I'd care to admit, honestly). I finally eliminated my stock versus broth confusion with a mnemonic device: the "b" in broth mirrors the "b" in "bits left behind." Maybe this will help you, too.

Homemade stock is another Southern pantry workhouse. In fact, it should be a staple of any kitchen, no matter where your longitude and latitude coordinates happen to fall. Additionally, since finding shelf-ready pork stock is a task of seemingly impossible proportions, making your own is a necessity. Pork stock marries perfectly with Southern foods and it really has no substitute. Put up several quarts of stock at once and your future self will be much obliged.

SERVING SUGGESTIONS

- *A well-crafted stock is the basis for all flavorful soups, stews, and other dishes. It serves as the foundation, providing backbone and strength to what would otherwise simply be water. Never underestimate its significance in creating truly delicious food.*
- *Use chicken stock as a base for chicken noodle soup.*
- *Use beef stock for an au jus for a French dip sandwich or as a base for pho.*
- *Use pork stock when making ramen or minestrone.*

STOCK (PORK, CHICKEN & BEEF)

· MAKES 2 TO 4 QUARTS ·

3 pounds beef or pork bones, or one 3- to 4-pound whole chicken

Salt and freshly ground black pepper

3 tablespoons extra-virgin olive oil (for chicken stock only)

2 onions, peeled and quartered

3 large carrots, peeled and halved

2 celery stalks with their leaves, roughly chopped

6 garlic cloves, peeled

4 bay leaves

1 teaspoon black peppercorns

4 sprigs fresh thyme

FOR PORK OR BEEF STOCK

1. Preheat the oven to 400°F. Place the pork or beef bones in a roasting pan and season them lightly on both sides with salt and pepper.

2. Place the pan in the oven and roast for 45 minutes, turning once, until the bones have caramelized and browned.

3. Remove the pan from the oven and transfer the bones to a large stockpot. Place the roasting pan over medium heat on the stovetop, and pour in about a cup of water to deglaze. Use a wooden spoon to scrape up any caramelized bits from the bottom of the pan. Pour this liquid into the stockpot.

4. Add the onions, carrots, celery, garlic, bay leaves, peppercorns, and thyme to the stockpot, as well as enough cold water to cover everything.

5. Gently simmer, uncovered, for 4 hours, topping off with water once or twice so that the ingredients are always fully covered.

6. Strain the stock through a fine-mesh sieve and then leave it to cool to room temperature. Transfer the cooled stock to lidded storage containers and either refrigerate and use within 4 to 5 days, or freeze and use within 3 to 4 months.

FOR CHICKEN STOCK

1. Preheat the oven to 450°F. Remove the giblets and neck from the chicken cavity; set aside for making stock. Rinse the chicken in cold water.

2. Using sharp kitchen scissors, cut the backbone out of the chicken and set it aside for stock.

3. Turn the chicken over and place it on a cutting board. Using your hands, press down hard on the breasts, to flatten the bird out a bit. Lay the chicken that way in a large roasting pan.

4. Coat the entire chicken with the olive oil. Sprinkle a bit of salt and several grinds of pepper over the surface of the bird.

5. Place the pan in the oven and roast for 45 minutes.

6. Test the chicken for doneness by placing a thermometer in the thickest part of the breast. When done, it should read at least 165°F. If it isn't done, return the pan to the oven for 5 to 15 minutes longer, depending on how close it was to the target temperature. Test again, returning to the oven for 5 minutes longer if necessary.

7. When the chicken is done, remove the pan from the oven. Lift up the chicken and set it on a cutting board to rest for about 15 minutes.

8. Place the roasting pan over medium heat on the stovetop, and pour in about a cup of water to deglaze. Use a wooden spoon to scrape up any caramelized bits from the bottom of the pan. Pour this liquid into a large stockpot.

9. Carve the chicken. Set the meat aside for another use. Place the carcass, reserved giblets, neck, and backbone into the stockpot. Proceed with steps 4 to 6 in the recipe for making Pork or Beef Stock.

GREASY RICE WITH PORK STOCK

· SERVES 4 ·

The components of this dish are misleadingly simple given the delicious outcome they produce when combined. A humble meal, put together in under an hour, as filling and satisfying as they come. You can opt to use breakfast sausage or ground pork, you'll just need to season up the latter with the Cajun Seasoning used in making Southern-Seasoned Potato Chips (page 160) if you go that route.

1 to 2 tablespoons Bacon Drippings (page 176)

1 pound ground pork or Breakfast Sausage (page 182)

1 tablespoon Cajun Seasoning, if using ground pork, otherwise omit (page 160)

1 onion, diced

2 carrots, diced

1 red bell pepper, diced

2 stalks celery, diced

3 garlic cloves, minced

1½ cups white rice

3 cups Pork Stock

1 teaspoon sea salt

Freshly ground black pepper

1 cup chopped celery leaves, parsley, and/or cilantro

Hot sauce, to serve (optional)

1. Warm a Dutch oven or large pot over medium heat. Add 1 tablespoon of bacon drippings. Once melted, add the sausage and cook for 6 minutes, until lightly browned. Remove the meat from the pan and set aside, leaving the fat behind in the pan.

2. Check the amount of bacon drippings in the pan; either add or remove drippings so that about 2 tablespoons remain. Add the onion, carrots, bell pepper, and celery. Sauté for 16 to 18 minutes, until the vegetables have browned around the edges.

3. Add the garlic and rice. Stir constantly for 5 minutes and then stir in the sausage.

4. Add the pork stock, salt, and several grinds of pepper. Cover the pot and simmer on low for about 20 minutes, stirring every 4 to 5 minutes.

5. Turn the heat off. Remove the lid, stir the rice, and then let sit with the lid on for 5 to 7 minutes. Taste for seasoning and then stir in the herbs. Serve with hot sauce, if desired.

CHICKEN & HERBED DUMPLINGS

· SERVES 4 ·

In the arena of chicken and dumplings, you can take one of two approaches: wide noodle or biscuit. While I grew up in a wide noodle household, I now prefer a biscuit dumpling (sorry, Mom!). As I can never get enough herbs, I found that adding them to the dumplings takes this Southern classic from tasty to transcendent.

6 cups Chicken Stock

1 teaspoon sea salt

Freshly ground black pepper

Meat from 1 roasted chicken, roughly cut into medium-size pieces

4 tablespoons Butter (page 194)

4 tablespoons all-purpose flour

FOR THE DUMPLINGS

1½ cups all-purpose flour

1½ teaspoons baking powder

1½ teaspoons sea salt

1 teaspoon chopped fresh rosemary

1 teaspoon chopped fresh thyme

1 teaspoon chopped fresh sage

3 tablespoons Butter, cubed (page 194)

¾ cup Buttermilk (page 199)

1. Warm a Dutch oven or large pot over medium-high heat. Add the stock, salt, and several grinds of pepper, and bring to a boil. Reduce the heat to low and add the chicken.
2. Melt the butter in a medium saucepan over medium heat. Whisking constantly, add in the flour and beat for 1 minute. Remove the pan from the heat, stir the roux into the stock mixture, and continue to simmer.
3. While the broth simmers, prepare the dumplings. Combine the flour, baking powder, salt, rosemary, thyme, and sage in a bowl and whisk until well combined.
4. Using a pastry cutter or two forks, cut in the butter until the mixture is crumbly and the butter is pea-size or smaller. Add the buttermilk and stir until the dough is just moistened and all the ingredients are combined.
5. Working quickly, pinch off tablespoon-size portions of the dough and drop them into the stock. Cover the pot and simmer for 15 to 17 minutes, until the dumplings are cooked through. Remove the pot from the heat. Ladle portions of the broth, meat, and dumplings into individual bowls and serve immediately (the dumplings will be quite hot).

WILD MUSHROOM BEEF STROGANOFF

· SERVES 4 TO 6 ·

This stroganoff is a dish to make when you have time. Which is to say, a lazy Sunday or planned potluck is ideal, while a busy weeknight is not. Most of it all happens in the slow cooker, though, so it's more of a waiting game than an active, stir-the-pot-at-all-times situation. If you have difficulty sourcing wild mushrooms (or lack the knowledge or an expert to help you source them safely), any type of mushrooms will do.

2 pounds chuck roast

1 large onion, roughly chopped

6 tablespoons Butter (page 194)

1 pound wild mushrooms or mushrooms of your choice, cut into large chunks

5 tablespoons all-purpose flour

3 cups Beef Stock, gently warmed

½ cup Buttermilk, gently warmed (page 199)

¼ cup bourbon

2 tablespoons spicy brown prepared mustard

1 tablespoon tomato paste

1 tablespoon Worcestershire sauce

2 teaspoons sea salt

Freshly ground black pepper

2 cups Sour Cream (page 207)

1 pound egg noodles, cooked

½ cup chopped fresh dill or parsley

1. Slice the chuck roast into ¼-inch-thick slices, no more than 3 inches long. Trim off any large segments of fat. Set the meat aside. Sear the fat in a saucepan for 5 minutes and then remove the seared pieces, leaving the liquid fat in the pan. Discard the pieces of fat (or give them to your dog!).

2. Add the onion to the saucepan and sauté for 10 minutes, until brown around the edges. Transfer the onion to a small bowl and set aside.

3. Melt 2 tablespoons of the butter in the pan. Add the mushrooms and sauté until all the liquid is gone and they start to stick a little to the bottom of the pan, 10 to 15 minutes. Transfer the mushrooms to a bowl and set aside.

4. Add the sliced meat to the pan and brown for 5 minutes. Remove both the meat and the juices and place in another bowl.

5. Melt the remaining 4 tablespoons butter in the saucepan and then stir in the flour for about 1 to 2 minutes, until it is an even blond roux. Splash a tiny bit of the stock into the roux, and stir to incorporate. Continue stirring, nonstop, while splashing a little more of the stock in at a time, until all of it has been added and is fully incorporated.

6. Stir in the juices from the meat, but not the meat yet. Add the buttermilk, bourbon, mustard, tomato paste, Worcestershire sauce, salt, and several grinds of pepper. Simmer over low heat for 20 minutes, stirring occasionally so that it does not stick to the pan.

7. Stir in the meat, onions, and mushrooms. Remove the pan from the heat, let cool for 5 minutes, and then transfer the contents to a slow cooker.

8. Cook on low for 5 hours. Transfer the mixture to a large pot or bowl. Stir in the sour cream until fully incorporated and then stir in the noodles and dill. Check the salt and adjust as necessary.

ICEBOX
— & —
FREEZER

BUTTER   **194**
     Brown Butter & Bourbon Braised Cabbage
     Mom's Fried Apples

BUTTERMILK   **199**
     Buttermilk & Smoky Paprika Fried Chicken
     Buttermilk Pancakes with Maple &
        Sorghum Syrup

CREAM CHEESE   **202**
     Shrimp & Cream Cheese Dip
     "Peaches & Cream" Tartines

SOUR CREAM   **207**
     Ambrosia with Lemon Verbena
     Sour Cream Bacon Dip

VANILLA ICE CREAM   **210**
     Bourbon Butter Pecan Ice Cream
     Peach Basil Ice Cream

BUTTER

A love, and use, of butter is nothing new. Stemming from the Greek word *boutyron*, loosely translated as "cow cheese" (from *bous* "ox or cow" and *tyros* "cheese"), butter appears in records as far back as 2000 B.C.E., indicating a global use of the creamy spread. The making of butter for household, trade, barter, or commercial use was historically the work of farmers' wives and milkmaids. Cream was placed in a plunger or dasher-style churn, and then hand agitated until the fat and liquid separated, forming butter and "buttermilk" (a wholly different beast from cultured buttermilk).

With the invention of the centrifuge by Swedish engineer Carl Gustaf Patrik de Laval, butter production began to make its way out of homes and cottage industries and into factories. The result was a greater amount of butter available for purchase, but a good deal of quality and flavor were compromised in the process.

Why make your own butter? Having authored a book on making homemade dairy products as well as regularly teaching classes on the topic, I've been asked this question more times than I can remember. It all comes down to flavor. Put simply, freshly made butter is astoundingly delicious. Plus, what would hot biscuits be without a healthy slathering? Or grits without a generous pat? Southern food and butter go hand in hand.

SERVING SUGGESTIONS

- *The fat of butter is exactly what lean foods like seafood and shellfish need to come alive. Melted butter served with cooked shrimp and crabmeat is truly transcendent.*
- *Butter is a key component in Pie Dough (page 217), Shortbread (page 225), Pound Cake (page 229), and Layer Cake (page 233).*
- *Keep a bit of butter at room temperature and slather liberally onto Buttermilk Pancakes with Maple & Sorghum Syrup (page 201).*
- *Mix with powdered sugar and vanilla extract to make buttercream frosting for cakes and cupcakes.*
- *Add the buttermilk drained off in the recipe to smoothies for a boost of creaminess.*

BUTTER

· MAKES ABOUT 1 CUP ·

1 pint heavy cream
¼ teaspoon salt (optional)

1. Let the cream come to room temperature, around 72°F to 74°F. Simply set the cream in a container on the kitchen counter, put a dairy thermometer into it, and check on it every 30 minutes or so until the temperature rises. This step lets the cream ripen a bit, raising its acidity, thereby making it easier to whip and pack with flavor.
2. Pour the cream into a food processor, secure the lid, and start running the machine.

3. The cream will begin to go through the butter-forming stages: sloshy, then stiff, and then separating into butter and buttermilk. Machine times vary, but it generally takes between 6 and 9 minutes (I average around 8).

4. Using a spatula, remove the butter from the machine. Place the buttery mass into a fine-mesh sieve set atop a bowl. Leave for a few minutes, allowing the liquid to drain off. Set the buttermilk aside for another use.

5. Transfer the butter to another bowl. Standing at the sink, start running cold water into the bowl. Empty the water out, and continue repeating several times until the water is clear in the bowl. Strain off any remaining water.

6. If you want to include salt, stir it in now with a metal spoon. Otherwise, put the butter mass on a cutting board.

7. Using a rubber spatula or wooden spoon, begin pressing the butter repeatedly, allowing any liquid trapped inside to drain off. Continue pressing until no liquid is visibly coming out when pressed.

8. Store at room temperature in a butter crock if you are planning to use your butter within 4 to 5 days. Or wrap in wax or parchment paper, or place in a container, and store in the refrigerator for up to 2 months or in the freezer for up to 6 months.

BROWN BUTTER & BOURBON BRAISED CABBAGE
· SERVES 4 ·

Several years ago, I attended a "Sunday Supper" at Rhubarb, a restaurant in downtown Asheville, North Carolina. A communally shared meal, Sunday Supper offers an opportunity to highlight a farm that the restaurant partners with and showcase their seasonal offerings. That night I ate a brown butter savory cabbage that instantly took me back to being sixteen years old and having dinner at the home of my friend Shannon Wallin. Her mom was braising cabbage in butter, and then served it alongside some meat entrée. I don't remember the meat, but I'll never forget that cabbage. Rhubarb's cabbage satisfied me in the same way, and a glug of bourbon only heightens the dish's memorable qualities in my version.

---

4 tablespoons Butter

1 medium green or Savoy cabbage, cut into bite-size pieces

½ cup bourbon

1 tablespoon lemon juice

1 teaspoon sea salt

1 Granny Smith, Honeycrisp, Winesap, Jonagold, or Braeburn apple, diced

1. Melt the butter in a medium saucepan over medium heat for 1 to 2 minutes, until lightly browned and emitting a pleasing, nutty aroma.

2. Add the cabbage to the pan and toss with a spatula or spoon until evenly coated. Cook for about 10 minutes, until the cabbage starts to brown around the edges a bit.

3. Add the bourbon, lemon juice, and salt, and cook for about 5 minutes. Stir in the diced apple, and cook for 5 minutes longer. Remove from the heat and serve.

MOM'S FRIED APPLES

· SERVES 4 ·

While workday breakfasts of my childhood consisted of a bowl of cold cereal or piece of toast, come the weekend, Mom would fry some bacon and eggs, bake a batch of biscuits, and cook these apples. More sautéed than fried, per se, Mom called them fried apples and the name stuck. Sweet, enrobed in just the right amount of fat, and peppered throughout with a hint of spice, these apples will always be welcome on my Southern table. Use an apple variety with firm, non-mealy flesh for best results.

2 tablespoons Butter

1 tablespoon Bacon Drippings (page 176)

8 firm apples, cored, quartered, and then cut into ½-inch slices (skins left on)

¼ cup granulated sugar

¼ cup packed light brown sugar

1 teaspoon ground cinnamon

½ teaspoon ground cloves

¼ teaspoon ground allspice

1. Warm the butter and drippings in a medium saucepan over medium-high heat.
2. Add the apples and use a spatula or spoon to fully coat them with the melted butter and drippings. Cover and cook over medium heat for 5 minutes.
3. Add the granulated sugar, brown sugar, cinnamon, cloves, and allspice, and stir to fully incorporate into the apples.
4. Continue tossing and stirring over medium-low heat for about 10 minutes, until the sugars caramelize, the water cooks off, and the apples are fragrant and becoming limp. Remove the pan from the heat and serve immediately.

BUTTERMILK

Buttermilk is a cultured dairy product. Which is to say, it has undergone fermentation. During fermentation of milk, naturally present bacteria interact with air, turning milk sugar (lactose) into lactic acid. These bacteria, when placed in a warm environment—such as the one you'll create when making buttermilk, yogurt, and other cultured dairy products—proliferate exponentially. The result is the telltale sour flavor associated with cultured dairy.

Almost up to her death in December 2015, my grandmother Nanny would ask whatever restaurant she was patronizing if they happened to have buttermilk on hand. She loved the creamy beverage, and would sip a glass of it with quiet contentment. Buttermilk is an essential element of a Southern foods kitchen, its sourness imparting a depth of flavor and nuance to dishes while also gently tenderizing any meat it is combined with. Whenever I work with it, I'm flooded with fond memories of Nanny.

SERVING SUGGESTIONS

- *Buttermilk and cornbread are made for each other, the sourness of the milk playing off the sweetness of the bread. Do as many senior Southerners do and pour some into a bowl, and then crumble Cornbread (page 142) over top.*
- *Enjoy ice cold, straight up (my Nanny's preferred means of consumption!).*
- *Use in making Buttermilk Biscuits (page 147) for a biscuit with tang and gumption!*
- *Make buttermilk ice cream or buttermilk cheesecake.*

BUTTERMILK

· MAKES ABOUT 4 CUPS ·

4 cups whole milk

1 packet dried buttermilk culture, or ⅔ cup
   cultured buttermilk

1. Warm the milk in a small pot over medium-high heat until it reaches 85°F.
2. Transfer the milk to a glass or ceramic container. With a metal whisk or spoon, stir in the buttermilk culture or buttermilk until fully combined.
3. Cover the container with a lid and leave to rest at room temperature for 12 hours.
4. Store the buttermilk in an airtight container in the refrigerator. Use within 1 to 2 weeks.

BUTTERMILK & SMOKY PAPRIKA FRIED CHICKEN

· SERVES 4 TO 6 ·

I will eat fried chicken hot, cold, and anywhere in between. Although I've had some delicious bites of it when dining out, it is, admittedly, never as good as when we make it at home. That's likely on account of the buttermilk and paprika brine we place the chicken in overnight. It results in the most moist, smoky, flavorful chicken. My husband, Glenn, is a bona fide fried chicken master, and knows the perfect way to achieve that gorgeous mahogany brown skin I so crave. Now you can impress your friends and loved ones just like he wows me.

2 cups Buttermilk

2 tablespoons Worcestershire sauce

2 tablespoons smoked or plain sea salt

1 tablespoon smoked paprika

Dash of hot sauce

3 pounds chicken drumsticks

3 cups peanut oil for frying

1 egg

2 cups all-purpose flour

2 teaspoons granulated garlic

Freshly ground black pepper

1. Whisk the buttermilk, Worcestershire sauce, 1 tablespoon of the salt, paprika, and hot sauce in a bowl until fully combined.

2. Place the chicken in a sealable food storage bag, or an appropriately sized dish, and pour the buttermilk brine over it. Seal the bag or cover the dish and leave to soak in the refrigerator for 6 to 12 hours (longer is better), turning occasionally.

3. Remove the chicken from the refrigerator and separate the chicken from the buttermilk, reserving the buttermilk in a mixing bowl.

4. Let the chicken sit at room temperature on a large plate or platter for about 10 minutes. Preheat the oven to 350°F.

5. Place a metal cooling rack over a large rimmed baking pan. Lay the chicken pieces on the rack and bake for 20 minutes. Remove the pan from the oven and set aside until cool to the touch, about 15 minutes.

6. When the chicken is cool enough to handle, heat about ¾ inch of peanut oil in a 12-inch cast iron skillet to about 310°F.

7. While the oil heats, whisk the egg into the reserved buttermilk mixture until fully combined.

8. Mix the flour, the remaining 1 tablespoon salt, garlic, and a dozen generous grinds of pepper in a shallow baking pan.

9. Holding the handle on a drumstick, dip it into the buttermilk mixture, then dredge it in the flour, and set it aside on a clean plate or platter. Repeat with all the pieces. If you like a thick crust, repeat the process.

10. Cook the chicken in batches, being careful not to overcrowd the pan. Turn the pieces every 2 minutes using long metal tongs, for about 12 minutes, until they are a deep, rich, reddish brown.

11. Set aside to cool on a wire rack for several minutes before serving.

BUTTERMILK PANCAKES WITH MAPLE & SORGHUM SYRUP

· SERVES 4 ·

Like most children, our son Huxley is a fan of pancakes. He requests them on the regular, most frequently when he asks what day it is and we tell him Saturday or Sunday. Though we work from home, we all still seem to associate the weekend with pancakes. We like ours with a buttermilk base, offering a slightly tangy contrast to the sweetness of the syrup.

FOR THE SYRUP

1 cup maple syrup

1 cup sorghum syrup

FOR THE PANCAKES

5 egg whites

2 cups all-purpose flour

½ cup fine-grind cornmeal

1 tablespoon baking powder

A pinch of sea salt

2 cups Buttermilk

4 egg yolks

Butter for cooking and for serving

1. Combine the maple and sorghum syrups in a small bowl. Set aside.
2. Either by hand or using an electric mixer, whip the egg whites until stiff. Set aside.
3. With a whisk or fork, stir the flour, cornmeal, baking powder, and salt in a medium bowl until fully combined. Add the buttermilk and egg yolks, and whisk until the mixture is completely smooth with no lumps. Gently fold in the egg whites until fully incorporated.
4. Liberally butter a cast iron skillet and warm over medium heat. Ladle the pancake batter in portions about the diameter of a grapefruit onto the pan. When the pancakes start to maintain their holes after they pop, flip them, adding more butter in between the flips if necessary. Cook for about 1 minute longer, and then remove from the pan. The pancakes should have crispy brown edges.
5. Serve immediately, or keep in a gently warmed oven until ready to serve. Enjoy with the syrup and butter.

CREAM CHEESE

———

The history of cream cheese stretches back millennia. Some historians claim that the ancient Greeks created it, serving the cheese to athletes competing in the first Olympic Games held in 776 B.C.E. Other anthropologists point to an even more far-reaching point of origin, having unearthed cheese molds dating to 2,000 B.C.E.

No matter who made it, cream cheese persists today for one simple reason: it is delicious. In addition to a welcome, mildly sour flavor, its creamy mouthfeel makes it highly appealing to sometimes finicky eaters such as children. Furthermore, it's highly versatile, working equally well in sweet and savory dishes.

Cream cheese made its way into Southern kitchens likely toward the end of the nineteenth century. American dairyman William Lawrence of Chester, New York, developed the cream cheese that is known today as Philadelphia brand when attempting to create the soft, spreadable French cheese Neufchâtel. As his creation gained popularity, it became a regular workhorse in kitchens across the nation.

Making the spreadable dairy item requires using a type of cheese culture called "direct-set mesophilic culture," as well as calcium chloride and liquid rennet. While you're unlikely to find these items on the shelves of your neighborhood grocery store, they can often be sourced at many natural foods stores, as well as from online retailers. It takes a bit of work and a bit of time to create this cheese, but, as it's said, good things come to those who wait. It's worth the effort, I guarantee you.

SERVING SUGGESTIONS

- *There may be no Southern snack more classic than cream cheese with Hot Pepper Jelly (page 82) spread onto a Saltine (page 85), the heat of the jelly offset by the creamy fat of the cheese. Serve with iced tea riddled with lemon wedges.*
- *Slather onto a toasted bagel and top with Bacon (page 176) crumbles and Chow Chow (page 19).*
- *Use to bake into a sweet or savory cheesecake (for a savory cheesecake swirl in a bit of Tomato Jam before baking, page 67).*

CREAM CHEESE

· MAKES ABOUT 1½ CUPS ·

---

3 cups whole milk

3 cups heavy cream

½ teaspoon (1 packet) direct-set mesophilic culture

¼ teaspoon calcium chloride mixed with ¼ cup cold water (see Note)

2 drops liquid rennet

NOTE: You may omit if using raw milk.

1. Combine the milk and cream in the top half of a double boiler or a metal bowl placed over a pot. Indirectly warm the mixture to 72°F.

2. Add the starter culture, and stir with a metal spoon to fully combine. Add the calcium chloride, if using, and stir for 1 minute.

3. Stir in the rennet. Remove the pot from the heat source, cover with a lid, and leave to rest at room temperature for 24 hours.

4. After the resting time, the mixture should resemble firm pieces of yogurt. Line a colander, drainer, or large sieve with butter muslin or a double layer of cheesecloth. Transfer the mixture and any liquid (the "whey") into the cloth-covered colander.

5. Tie the four corners of the cloth together into a knot. Suspend the bag over the kitchen sink faucet, or thread a wooden spoon or dowel through the knot and suspend the bag over a catch bowl. Drain for 10 hours at room temperature.

6. Once you no longer see any whey dripping from the bag, remove the curds from the cloth and store in a lidded container.

7. Chill for at least 1 hour before serving. Store in the refrigerator and use within 1 to 2 weeks.

SHRIMP & CREAM CHEESE DIP

· MAKES ABOUT 2½ CUPS ·

Dips were an indispensable part of my upbringing. Potato chips, crackers—we dunked nearly everything we could into dips. This dip is a tribute to the two high school years I spent living in Morehead City, North Carolina, a coastal town with a vibrant and active seafood industry, and where shrimping is a way of life.

---

1 pound shrimp, peeled and deveined

2 large stalks celery, diced

2 tablespoons extra-virgin olive oil

1 teaspoon plus a pinch sea salt

1½ cups Cream Cheese

2 tablespoons minced fresh dill

1 teaspoon granulated garlic

¼ cup Sweet Pickle Relish (page 30)

1 tablespoon lemon juice

1 cup packed celery leaves, cilantro, or parsley (or a blend of all three)

Freshly ground black pepper

1. Preheat the oven to 400°F. Toss the shrimp and celery with the olive oil and a pinch of salt on a large rimmed baking sheet. Spread out evenly and roast for 6 to 8 minutes, until the shrimp are pink and cooked through. Remove the pan from the oven and set aside to cool for about 6 to 7 minutes.

2. Cut each shrimp into three pieces. Place the shrimp, celery, and cream cheese in a medium bowl and stir to combine. Stir in the dill, garlic, relish, the remaining 1 teaspoon of salt, lemon juice, celery leaves, and several grinds of pepper.

3. Cover the mixture and place in the refrigerator. Chill for at least 30 minutes before serving with your choice of chips or crackers.

"PEACHES & CREAM" TARTINES

· SERVES 6 ·

Much like the Southern Tartines with Roasted Brussels Sprouts on page 70, this open-faced sandwich is loaded with fresh ingredients. A wee bit of salty country ham acts as a counterbalance to the sweetness of the honeyed cream cheese and peaches. A perfect summertime snack.

1 cup Cream Cheese, room temperature

1 tablespoon honey

½ teaspoon vanilla extract

6 pieces toast

2 peaches, sliced

1 cucumber, seeded and sliced into crescents

4 ounces cooked country ham, sliced into
  bite-size strips

A handful of fresh mint leaves

Freshly ground black pepper (optional)

1. Combine the cream cheese, honey, and vanilla in a bowl.

2. Spread the cream cheese mixture evenly on the toast. Top with the peaches, cucumber, ham, mint leaves, and several grinds of black pepper, if using. Serve immediately.

SOUR CREAM

One of the most fascinating and enlightening parts of researching this book was all the unexpected food route history I discovered. Things that I thought were intrinsically "American" turned out to be anything but. Take sour cream, for instance. If you think it's as American as apple pie, or perhaps a product of Mexico due to its frequent pairing with burritos and tacos, think again.

Turns out we have the Mongols to thank for this sour condiment. While they didn't keep cows on their cold and steep terrain, they did keep herds of horses. From these horses, they made a type of fermented beverage from their milk. As the Mongols and their armies moved through Eurasia, this beverage spread with their conquests. Europeans began to incorporate the drink into their culinary repertoire, replacing the horse milk with cow's milk. The drink was also made thicker in its new incarnation, resulting in modern day sour cream. As Eastern Europeans moved west, immigrating across the Atlantic, their soured cream came with them.

In my Southern kitchen today, and in the one of my upbringing, there is and was always sour cream. From dips to baked potatoes, from tacos to stroganoff, it is a high-demand kitchen staple. Making your own is a great way to use up surplus buttermilk, should you find yourself in such a situation.

SERVING SUGGESTIONS

- *Sour cream and potatoes have a natural affinity, as neutral potatoes call for a stronger flavor to amp them up. Use as a baked potato topping, alongside Bacon crumbles (page 176) and minced chives.*
- *Dollop onto potato pancakes or hash browns.*
- *Sour cream is a key component of Wild Mushroom Beef Stroganoff (page 191). I love it so much in the dish that I even stir in a little extra at serving time.*

SOUR CREAM
· MAKES ABOUT 1 CUP ·

---

1 cup heavy cream
¼ cup Buttermilk (page 199)

1. Warm the cream in a small pot over medium-high heat until it reaches 85°F.
2. Transfer the cream to a glass or ceramic container. With a metal whisk or spoon, stir in the buttermilk until fully combined.
3. Cover the container with a lid and leave to rest at room temperature for 12 hours.
4. After the resting time, your mixture should have noticeably thickened. Store in a lidded container in the refrigerator and use within 1 to 2 weeks.

AMBROSIA WITH LEMON VERBENA

· SERVES 4 ·

For many, ambrosia is synonymous with white pools of oozy liquid, studded throughout with mini marshmallows, tinned fruit cocktail, and the need for a dose of a certain effervescent antacid shortly following its consumption. Not so with my ambrosia. For several years in my late twenties, I managed a bed-and-breakfast in western North Carolina. On occasion, when the owners were out of town, I'd inn-sit, which entailed making breakfast. It was then that I began "taking back ambrosia," so to speak, replacing its nearly unpalatable (to me, at least) format with a fresh, natural, delicious one for the inn's guests. Ripe fruits, sour cream, fresh herbs, and a bit of almond extract make for an ambrosia that's sure to delight, not derail.

½ pineapple, peeled, cored, and cut into chunks

1 orange, peeled and segments roughly chopped

1 cup strawberries, chopped

½ cup shredded sweetened coconut

1 cup Sour Cream

1 teaspoon almond extract

2 tablespoons minced fresh lemon verbena, lemon balm, or lemon thyme

1. Combine the pineapple, orange, strawberries, coconut, sour cream, and almond extract in a bowl and stir until well incorporated.
2. Cover the bowl and leave to chill in the refrigerator for 1 hour.
3. At serving time, evenly distribute the ambrosia among four bowls or serving glasses and top with lemon verbena.

SOUR CREAM BACON DIP

· MAKES ABOUT 2 CUPS ·

This is a bacon dip that my mom would seriously get behind, lover of dips as she is. It is creamy and salty and smoky and everything that a dip should be. Fry up a batch of Potato Chips (page 157), turn on the game (or awards show, if you're me), and dip into bliss.

6 pieces thick-cut, smoked Bacon (page 176)

1 cup chopped ramps or scallions

2 cups Sour Cream

1. Preheat the oven to 400°F. Place a metal cooling rack over a large rimmed baking sheet. Lay the bacon slices on the cooling rack and bake for 15 minutes, until browned and fragrant. Once cool to the touch, crumble into small pieces.

2. Pour off 2 tablespoons of bacon fat from the baking sheet into a medium saucepan. Sauté the ramps in the bacon fat for about 5 minutes over low heat, until cooked through. Remove the pan from the heat, and set aside to cool for 6 to 7 minutes.

3. Transfer the ramps to a food processor. Add the bacon and sour cream and process until fully combined. If you don't have a food processor, you can use a blender; or simply chop the ramps and bacon as finely as possible by hand and stir them into the sour cream.

VANILLA ICE CREAM

Growing up, I associated ice cream with church socials or with my maternal grandmother, Nanny. The concept of an ice cream social as a means of entertainment developed in the United States in the nineteenth century. French confectioners that had relocated to the United States after the French Revolution started producing ice cream for the public in outdoor settings known as "ice cream gardens." Since women, female youth, and children at the time were prohibited from visiting the taverns and pubs that males enjoyed, ice cream gardens became popular locations for the well-to-do to socialize, children to play, and folks to flirt in a benign setting.

As advances were made in industrial manufacturing, refrigeration, and freezing, commercially produced ice cream gained in production scale. As a result, manufacturing costs went down, making ice cream more affordable. Ice cream gardens as a socializing location of the elite became less common. The concept of an ice cream social was then appropriated by churches, typically in the form of fundraising events, which is how I, as a church-going youth, drew a parallel between ice cream and church.

We often joked that my grandmother's favorite food group was ice cream. She would talk about having a hollow leg that enabled her to save room for ice cream even when she'd eaten her fill at mealtime. Homemade vanilla ice cream is a joy that everyone should experience at least once. I hope you enjoy it numerous times. I have no doubt Nanny would approve.

SERVING SUGGESTIONS

- *All on its own, ice cream is simply sweet and creamy. If you add in some stronger flavors and textures, however, including those with a bit of bitterness, all that sweetness gets properly tempered. Drizzle with sorghum or maple syrup and top with Candied Black Walnuts (page 164).*
- *Serve a scoop or two alongside Pound Cake (page 229), and top with seasonal fresh fruit or Canned Stone Fruits (page 128).*
- *Ice cream and warm sonkers are sublime together. Serve à la mode with one of the sonker options in the book (pages 221 to 224) or create a version of your own.*

VANILLA ICE CREAM

· MAKES ABOUT 6 CUPS ·

3 cups whole milk

2 cups heavy cream

⅔ cup sugar

½ teaspoon sea salt

1 teaspoon vanilla extract

5 large egg yolks, beaten

1. Combine the milk, cream, sugar, salt, and vanilla in a large saucepan. Whisk over medium heat, stirring frequently, until the sugar fully dissolves, about 5 minutes.

2. Remove about ½ cup of the mixture from the pan, and gradually whisk it into the egg yolks. Slowly whisk the warmed yolk blend back into the saucepan. Whisking continuously, cook

about 8 to 10 minutes, until the custard thickens and coats the back of a spoon. Remove the saucepan from the heat.

3. Strain the mixture through a fine-mesh sieve set atop a bowl. Cover the bowl and place it in the refrigerator for 8 to 12 hours.

4. Place the custard into the bowl of an electric ice cream machine, and process according to the model's manufacturing instructions. Transfer to a lidded container and freeze for at least 2 hours before serving. Consume within 7 to 10 days.

BOURBON BUTTER PECAN ICE CREAM

· MAKES ABOUT 7 CUPS ·

That regrettable foray into bubblegum ice cream notwithstanding, I've had two favorite ice cream flavors since I was about seven years old: coffee and butter pecan. Those preferences have stuck with me for decades, and are just as true today as they were in the mid-eighties. Only difference these days is a splash of coffee liqueur in my coffee ice cream and a tipple of bourbon in my butter pecan, as detailed here.

---

3 cups whole milk

2 cups heavy cream

⅔ cup sugar

½ teaspoon sea salt

1 teaspoon vanilla extract

5 large egg yolks, beaten

FOR THE PECANS

2 cups chopped pecans

½ cup bourbon

3 tablespoons salted butter

¼ cup sorghum syrup

½ teaspoon smoked or plain sea salt

1. Combine the milk, cream, sugar, salt, and vanilla in a large saucepan. Whisk over medium heat, stirring frequently, until the sugar fully dissolves, about 5 minutes.

2. Remove about ½ cup of the mixture from the pan, and gradually whisk it into the egg yolks. Slowly whisk the warmed yolk blend back into the saucepan. Whisking continuously, cook about 8 to 10 minutes, until the custard thickens and coats the back of a spoon. Remove the saucepan from the heat.

3. Strain the mixture through a fine-mesh sieve set atop a bowl. Cover the bowl and place it in the refrigerator for 8 to 12 hours.

4. **PREPARE THE PECANS.** Warm a medium saucepan over medium-low heat and toast the pecans for 2 minutes, stirring frequently. Add the bourbon, stir for 1 minute, then add the butter and stir until melted. Add the sorghum and the salt. Cook for 2 to 3 minutes, until the sorghum is no longer runny.

5. Spoon the nuts onto a parchment-lined baking sheet. Set aside until completely cool to the touch.

6. Place the custard into the bowl of an electric ice cream machine. Process for 5 minutes, and then add the pecan pieces. Continue processing as per the model's manufacturing instructions.

7. Transfer to a lidded container and freeze for at least 2 hours before serving. Consume within 7 to 10 days.

PEACH BASIL ICE CREAM

· MAKES ABOUT 7 CUPS ·

Peaches and basil are a natural pairing. They are as delicious in a peach-centric caprese salad as they are incorporated into vanilla ice cream. The basil will darken once minced but the color change won't affect its flavor.

3 cups whole milk

2 cups heavy cream

2/3 cup sugar

1/2 teaspoon sea salt

1 teaspoon vanilla extract

5 large egg yolks, beaten

1 1/2 cups chopped ripe peaches

2 tablespoons minced fresh basil

1. Combine the milk, cream, sugar, salt, and vanilla in a large saucepan. Whisk over medium heat, stirring frequently, until the sugar fully dissolves, about 5 minutes.

2. Remove about 1/2 cup of the mixture from the pan, and gradually whisk it into the egg yolks. Slowly whisk the warmed yolk blend back into the saucepan. Whisking continuously, cook about 8 to 10 minutes, until the custard thickens and coats the back of a spoon. Remove the saucepan from the heat.

3. Strain the mixture through a fine-mesh sieve set atop a bowl. Cover the bowl and place it in the refrigerator for 8 to 12 hours.

4. Place the custard into the bowl of an electric ice cream machine. Process for 5 minutes, and then add the peaches and basil. Continue processing as per the model's manufacturing instructions.

5. Transfer to a lidded container and freeze at least 2 hours before serving. Consume within 7 to 10 days.

SWEETENERS
— & —
DESSERTS

PIE DOUGH

———

Where would the South be without pie? I cannot thank the Pilgrims enough for bringing this culinary treasure with them when they sailed to the New World. Initially, pies were a savory food, packed with venison and wild game, similar to those made back in England. It is believed that Native Americans introduced sweet fillings, in the form of fruits and berries.

Though the introduction of sweet fillings occurred in the seventeenth century, paving the way for the multitudinous offerings of sweet pies today, pie dough wasn't given much thought until many decades later. The dough was hard, even inedible, intended merely as the vehicle for the pie's fillings, not as a product to be consumed itself. Recipes from the eighteenth century reflect a change in approach, with pie dough becoming an edible component of the pie itself.

I honed this pie dough recipe over the course of writing my book on seasonal sweet and savory pies, *A Year of Pies*. When you author a book on pie-making, you get ample opportunity to tweak your pie dough. This pie dough has never failed me. Buttery and flaky, it has garnered countless compliments over the years. The chill time is crucial, as cold dough into a hot oven is what ensures flakiness. May it serve as your launchpad for the Southern pies of your dreams.

SERVING SUGGESTIONS

- *Pie dough is like a blank slate. It is a sturdy, buttery base upon which to heap flavorful toppings. To that end, I encourage you to use it in a beef or vegetarian shepherd's pie, topped with buttery mounds of Yukon gold mashed potatoes.*
- *In a similar savory vein, use pie dough to create hand-held meat pies. Watermelon Rind Sloppy Joes (page 49) would be delicious in this format.*
- *If you have any leftover dough, pack it into mini muffin tins, top with jam or jelly, and bake at 350°F for 10 to 15 minutes.*

———

PIE DOUGH

· MAKES 2 PIE DOUGH DISKS ·

———

2½ cups all-purpose flour	1 cup Butter, chilled and cubed (page 194)
1¼ teaspoons salt	¾ cup ice water

1. Mix the flour and salt together in a medium-large bowl.
2. Using a pastry cutter or two forks, cut in the butter until the mixture begins to look crumbly but some pea-size chunks of butter still remain.
3. Slowly drizzle in the ice water. Stir with a mixing spoon until the dough starts to clump.

4. Transfer the dough onto a floured work surface, and fold it together into itself using your hands. The dough should come together easily but should not feel overly sticky. Flour your hands as needed to prevent the dough from sticking to you.

5. Cut the dough in half and shape into two balls. Wrap each dough ball in plastic wrap and refrigerate for at least 1 hour.

6. Proceed according to the recipe instructions. Alternatively, store the dough disks in an airtight container or zippered freezer bag in the refrigerator for up to 1 week or in the freezer for up to 6 months (you'll need to move the dough out of the freezer and into the refrigerator 24 hours before you plan to use it).

SORGHUM BOURBON ORANGE PECAN PIE
· MAKES ONE 9-INCH PIE ·

In theory, I love the idea of pecan pie. In reality, however, it's typically far beyond my sweetness threshold. Instead, I prefer a sorghum pecan pie. Its sweetness is subtler, less defined by aching cavities than by sweet tooth appeasement. I've added bourbon and orange zest to bump up the flavor interest.

1 disk Pie Dough

2 cups pecans

5 tablespoons Butter (page 194)

⅔ cup packed light brown sugar

⅔ cup sorghum syrup

½ teaspoon sea salt

4 eggs, room temperature, beaten

3 tablespoons bourbon

2 teaspoons vanilla extract

Zest of 1 orange

1. **PREPARE THE CRUST**. Remove the dough from the refrigerator. Roll it out on a lightly floured surface to an 11- to 12-inch circle.

2. Fit the dough into a 9-inch pie pan and trim the overhang to 1 inch. Crimp the edges decoratively, if desired.

3. Place the crust in the refrigerator while you prepare the filling.

4. **PREPARE THE FILLING**. Preheat the oven to 350°F. Spread the pecans evenly across a large rimmed baking sheet. Toast for 10 minutes, flipping the nuts over halfway through, until slightly darkened and fragrant. Remove the pan from the oven, dump the nuts onto a cutting board, and leave to cool for 10 minutes. Once cool enough to handle, roughly chop the pecans.

5. Melt the butter, brown sugar, sorghum, and salt in a medium saucepan over medium heat. Remove the pan from the heat and whisk in the eggs, bourbon, and vanilla. Stir in the orange zest and chopped pecan pieces.

6. **ASSEMBLE THE PIE**. Pour the filling into the chilled crust, using a spatula to distribute it evenly.

7. Bake at 350°F for 40 to 45 minutes, until the pie is set in the center; it shouldn't wobble or jiggle when you touch the pan. Cool fully to room temperature before serving.

"OLD FASHIONED" SWEET POTATO PIE

· MAKES ONE 9-INCH PIE ·

A play on the Old Fashioned cocktail, which partners liquor with bitters and orange, this is my adult version of a classic sweet potato pie. Separating the egg whites and yolks helps produce a lighter, fluffier pie.

1 disk Pie Dough

FOR THE FILLING
3 pounds sweet potatoes
4 eggs, yolks and whites separated
1 cup heavy cream
4 tablespoons Butter, cubed (page 194)
½ cup bourbon
¼ cup maple syrup

¼ cup light brown sugar, packed
1 teaspoon sea salt
Grated peel of 2 oranges
3 dashes bitters (such as Angostura)
1 teaspoon orange extract

FOR THE EGG WASH
1 large egg yolk
1 tablespoon cold water

1. **PREPARE THE CRUST**. Remove the dough from the refrigerator. Roll it out on a lightly floured surface to an 11- to 12-inch circle.
2. Fit the dough into a 9-inch pie pan and trim the overhang to 1 inch. Crimp the edges decoratively, if desired.
3. Place the crust in the refrigerator while you prepare the filling.
4. **PREPARE THE SWEET POTATOES**. Preheat the oven to 400°F. Prick each potato three or four times with a fork.
5. Line a rimmed baking sheet with parchment paper. Place the potatoes on the sheet and bake for 1 hour, until easily pierced with a fork. Remove the pan from the oven and reduce the oven temperature to 350°F.
6. Cool the potatoes for 10 to 15 minutes, until they can be handled. Peel the skins off.
7. Put the potatoes into a food processor, purée until smooth, and transfer to a medium mixing bowl. Alternatively, mash them in a large bowl with a potato masher until fully softened and silky.
8. **PREPARE THE FILLING**. With an electric mixer, beat the egg whites until billowy peaks form. Set aside.
9. Add the heavy cream and butter to the mashed sweet potatoes. Whisk until the butter melts and the cream is well incorporated, then whisk in the egg yolks until fully combined.
10. Place the bourbon in a medium saucepan. Bring to a boil over high heat, boil for 1 to 2 minutes, and then stir in the maple syrup and brown sugar. Remove the pan from the heat and pour into the potato mixture. Whisk until well combined.
11. Add the salt, orange peel, bitters, and orange extract. Whisk until all the ingredients are fully blended.
12. With a spatula, gently fold the egg whites into the sweet potato mixture until the whites are fully incorporated.

13. **ASSEMBLE THE PIE**. Pour the filling into the chilled piecrust, using a spatula to distribute it evenly.

14. Whisk together the egg yolk and water in a small bowl, then use a pastry brush to brush the wash over the edges of the crust.

15. Bake in the 350°F oven for 60 to 70 minutes, until the filling is set and doesn't jiggle when the pie pan is gently shaken.

16. Cool for at least 1 hour before serving, so the pie has time to set up and firm throughout.

BUTTERMILK CHERRY PIE

· MAKES ONE 9-INCH PIE ·

The secret to this pie, in my estimation, is the fresh vanilla bean seeds. Easily found at natural foods stores and in the baking section of most grocery stores, fresh vanilla beans offer a flavor and aroma that can only be described as ambrosial. Combined with puckery buttermilk and sweet cherries, a slice of this pie will make anyone smile.

---

1 disk Pie Dough

6 tablespoons Butter, melted (page 194)

1 cup sugar

¼ cup all-purpose flour

2 eggs, beaten

1 cup Buttermilk (page 199)

Pinch of sea salt

1 vanilla bean, split and seeded

½ pound sweet cherries, stemmed and pitted

1. **PREPARE THE CRUST**. Preheat the oven to 400°F.

2. Remove the dough from the refrigerator. Roll it out on a lightly floured surface to an 11- to 12-inch circle.

3. Fit the dough into a 9-inch pie pan and trim the overhang to 1 inch. Crimp the edges decoratively, if desired.

4. Prick the bottom of the crust six or seven times with a fork. Place the crust in the refrigerator for 15 minutes.

5. Line the piecrust with parchment and fill it with dried beans or pie weights.

6. Bake for 10 to 12 minutes, then remove the pan from the oven and reduce the oven temperature to 350°F.

7. Remove the dried beans or pie weights and parchment. Cool the crust completely before filling.

8. **PREPARE THE FILLING**. Whisk the butter and sugar in a medium mixing bowl until fully combined. Add the flour, and whisk until no lumps are present.

9. Whisk in the eggs, buttermilk, salt, and vanilla bean seeds and whisk until the mixture is completely uniform in consistency.

10. **ASSEMBLE THE PIE**. Pour the egg mixture into the prepared piecrust. Gently distribute the cherries across the surface.

11. Bake at 350°F for 50 to 60 minutes, just until the edges of the pie are set and firm but the center is still a bit jiggly (it will firm up as it cools).

12. Remove the pie from the oven. Set aside to cool for at least 1 hour before serving.

SONKER

A dish native to Mount Airy, North Carolina, sonkers are a deep-dish cobbler-like pie made with any kind of fruit. Historically, they were baked on farms to make use of whatever fruit was currently abundant and in season in order to feed all the farm workers. Some sonkers have a pie dough–like topping, while others have a more dolloped, biscuit-y topping. Sonker toppings offer a fluffy, airy, somewhat neutral contrast to their sweet fillings below. They balance out a dish in the manner that flour rounds out a batch of cookies or a cake, by giving it both substance and a departure from pure sweetness.

I had never heard of sonker, to be honest, until I began research for my book *A Year of Pies*. While crisps, buckles, slumps, grunts, betties, and cobblers are known across the United States, the term "sonker" as a dessert description seems to be limited to Surrey and Wilkes counties in North Carolina. Few have heard of it beyond the region.

What follows is my recipe for sonker topping, along with two means of employing it. As already mentioned, the whole point of sonker is to use whatever fruit is in season and abundantly available so feel free to make substitutions as desired.

SERVING SUGGESTIONS

- *Open a jar of Canned Stone Fruits (page 128), pour into a buttered baking dish, top with the sonker topping, and bake according to the instructions listed for the other sonker recipes (pages 221 to 224).*
- *Use nectarines or apricots and basil instead of peaches and lavender in Peach Lavender Sonker (page 222).*
- *Swap in blueberries for the blackberries in Blackberry Lemon Sonker (page 222).*

SONKER

· MAKES ENOUGH FOR ONE 10-INCH SKILLET OR 9-INCH PIE PAN ·

---

1 cup all-purpose flour	¼ teaspoon sea salt
1 teaspoon baking powder	3 tablespoons Butter, cubed (page 194)
¼ teaspoon baking soda	¾ cup Buttermilk (page 199)

1. Combine the flour, baking powder, baking soda, and salt in a medium bowl.
2. Using a pastry cutter or two forks, cut in the butter until the mixture is crumbly and the butter is pea-size or smaller.
3. Create a well in the center of the mixture and pour in the buttermilk.
4. Using a mixing spoon, gently incorporate the buttermilk just until all the dry ingredients are moistened. The mixture will look quite wet at this point, but that's fine.
5. Proceed according to the recipe instructions.

BLACKBERRY LEMON SONKER

· MAKES ONE 10-INCH SKILLET OR 9-INCH PIE PAN ·

If you opt for a skillet on this sonker or the next one, be sure it's an enamel-coated one. Otherwise, the flavor of the iron in the skillet will soon permeate the fruit, rendering it metallic-tasting. I learned this the hard way after baking several sonkers that tasted great the first 20 or so minutes out of the oven, but then become "funky" as they sat in the pan.

4½ half-pints blackberries (6 ounces each)

1 cup sugar

¼ cup arrowroot powder or cornstarch

2 tablespoons all-purpose flour

Zest of 1 lemon

Sonker Topping

3 tablespoons Butter, melted (page 194)

1. Preheat the oven to 425°F. Butter a 10-inch enamel-coated skillet or a 9-inch pie pan.
2. Combine the blackberries, sugar, arrowroot powder, flour, and lemon zest in a medium bowl. Stir until the ingredients are fully combined and the blackberries are well coated.
3. Cover the bowl with a kitchen cloth and set aside for 15 minutes. Meanwhile, prepare the sonker topping.
4. Fill the prepared pan with the blackberry mixture. Using a spoon, dollop the sonker topping onto the surface of the berries, aiming for mounds of about 3 tablespoons. You needn't be terribly specific on the amount; as long as the surface is dotted with small mounds, you're in good shape.
5. Pour the melted butter over the sonker topping. Bake at 425°F for 15 minutes. Reduce the oven temperature to 350°F and continue baking for 30 minutes longer.
6. Cool for at least 30 minutes before serving.

PEACH LAVENDER SONKER

· MAKES ONE 10-INCH SKILLET OR 9-INCH PIE PAN ·

Mountain Farm is a lavender, goat, and blueberry farm in Burnsville, North Carolina, that used to host a lavender festival each Father's Day. My husband, our son Huxley, and I would attend annually, celebrating the holiday with a picnic and all manner of lavender delights produced by the farm. Though they've since done away with the festival, Mountain Farm still grows and sells lavender, which I incorporated into this sonker, my homage to all that is sweet and fragrant about summer.

2 to 3 pounds peaches, peeled, pitted, and
    cut into ¼-inch slices (about 4 cups)

1 cup sugar

¼ cup arrowroot powder or cornstarch

2 tablespoons all-purpose flour

1 tablespoon dried or 2 tablespoons fresh
    lavender buds

Sonker Topping

3 tablespoons Butter, melted (page 194)

1. Preheat the oven to 425°F. Butter a 10-inch enamel-coated skillet or a 9-inch pie pan.

2. Combine the peaches, sugar, arrowroot powder, flour, and lavender buds in a medium bowl. Stir until the ingredients are fully combined and the peach slices are well coated.

3. Cover the bowl with a kitchen cloth and set aside for 15 minutes. Meanwhile, prepare the sonker topping.

4. Fill the prepared pan with the peach mixture. Using a spoon, dollop the sonker topping onto the surface of the peaches, aiming for mounds of about 3 tablespoons. You needn't be terribly specific on the amount; as long as the surface is dotted with small mounds, you're in good shape.

5. Pour the melted butter over the sonker topping. Bake at 425°F for 15 minutes. Reduce the oven temperature to 350°F and continue baking for 30 minutes longer.

6. Cool for at least 30 minutes before serving.

SHORTBREAD

———

I cannot recall exactly the age that I became obsessed with all things Scotland. I may have been around twenty years old when my friend Dustan first introduced to me the film *My Dinner with Andre*, wherein Andre recounts his time at Findhorn, an intentional community in Scotland. It might have been through a college boyfriend's British mother who was always receiving packages of goodies from her own mother back in England. Shortbread, Scotland's dessert creation, was nearly always among the treasures. Or perhaps it was through my father's wife, or even my father, both lovers of shortbread and all things U.K.

Waves of Scotch-Irish immigrants began arriving in America in the late 1600s. Though they landed largely in Pennsylvania, many made their way south to the Shenandoah Valley of Virginia in the 1720s and, later, in the 1780s, to western North Carolina. Their influence has remained, as evidenced by folk traditions, cultural traits, and foods present in the region today, including shortbread.

Since 2008, I have hosted an annual ladies' cookie exchange in early December at my home. Though each year I vow to branch out and bake something different, I can't help myself from returning to shortbread time after time. It is delicious, easy to bake, forgiving, and accommodating of nearly any flavor pairings I ply it with. A go-to shortbread recipe should be in the kitchen of any Southern baker, Scotland devotee or not. Here's mine.

SERVING SUGGESTIONS

- *Shortbread is sturdy and flavorful, making it an ideal foundation for a dessert. Render the shortbread into fine crumbs, toss with a bit of melted butter, spread into a springform pan, and use as the base for a tart.*
- *I think shortbread is pretty much perfection all on its own, but you might consider serving some with a pot of strongly brewed Earl Grey tea for a delightful afternoon treat.*
- *Crumble the cookies into large pieces and serve with Banana Pudding (page 232) and seasonal, fresh fruit.*

———

SHORTBREAD

· MAKES 2 DOZEN ·

———

2 cups all-purpose flour	½ teaspoon sea salt
½ cup sugar	1 cup Butter, cut into chunks (page 194)

1. Pulse the flour, sugar, and salt together in a food processor until combined. Add the butter and pulse until the mixture begins to come together and hold its shape. This will take about 1 to 2 minutes, so don't worry if the mixture looks crumbly at first.
2. Divide the dough in half. Set one half on a sheet of parchment paper, shape it into a 6-inch log, and roll it up in the parchment. Repeat with the second half of dough. Place both parchment-wrapped logs in the refrigerator and chill for 1 to 2 hours.

3. Preheat the oven to 300°F. Line two cookie sheets with parchment paper or silicone baking mats. Remove the dough logs from the refrigerator. Slice each log into 12 rounds, about ½-inch thick each.

4. Bake for 30 to 35 minutes, until the edges just begin to brown. Cool the shortbread for 5 minutes in the pan, and then transfer to wire cooling racks to cool completely. Transfer to an airtight lidded container. Consume within 7 to 10 days. .

CHOCOLATE-DIPPED ORANGE SHORTBREAD

· MAKES 2 DOZEN ·

Shortbread dipped in chocolate will instantly placate crabby children and cantankerous adults alike. Pair with a well-steeped mug of Earl Grey or a press pot of French roast for an afternoon delight.

---

2 cups all-purpose flour

½ cup sugar

½ teaspoon sea salt

1 cup Butter, cut into chunks (page 194)

Zest of 1 orange

1 cup (about 6 ounces) baking chocolate
 (at least 60% cocoa content)

1. Pulse the flour, sugar, and salt together in a food processor until combined. Add the butter and orange zest, and pulse until the mixture begins to come together and hold its shape. This will take about 1 to 2 minutes, so don't worry if the mixture looks crumbly at first.

2. Divide the dough in half. Set one half on a sheet of parchment paper, shape it into a 6-inch log, and roll it up in the parchment. Repeat with the second half of dough. Place both parchment-wrapped logs in the refrigerator and chill for 1 to 2 hours.

3. Preheat the oven to 300°F. Line two cookie sheets with parchment paper or silicone baking mats. Remove the dough logs from the refrigerator. Slice each log into 12 rounds, about ½-inch thick each.

4. Bake for 30 to 35 minutes, until the edges just begin to brown. Cool the shortbread for 5 minutes in the pan, and then transfer to wire cooling racks to cool completely.

5. Melt the chocolate in a double boiler or a microwave. Dip half of the shortbread in the chocolate, shake off any excess drips, and place on wax paper or a silicone baking mat. Set aside to harden. Store in an airtight lidded container and consume within 1 week.

CORNMEAL, LEMON & SAGE SHORTBREAD

· MAKES 2 DOZEN ·

Cornmeal and sage have long been incorporated into Southern kitchens. The brightness of lemon naturally complements the two, creating a shortbread that is at once sweet, earthy, and zesty.

1½ cups all-purpose flour

½ cup fine-grind cornmeal

½ cup sugar

½ teaspoon sea salt

1 cup Butter, cut into chunks (page 194)

3 tablespoons minced fresh sage (or
   1 tablespoon dried rubbed sage)

Zest of 1 lemon

1. Pulse the flour, cornmeal, sugar, and salt together in a food processor until combined. Add the butter, sage, and lemon zest, and pulse until the mixture begins to come together and hold its shape. This will take about 1 to 2 minutes, so don't worry if the mixture looks crumbly at first.

2. Divide the dough in half. Set one half on a sheet of parchment paper, shape it into a 6-inch log, and roll it up in the parchment. Repeat with the second half of dough. Place both parchment-wrapped logs in the refrigerator and chill for 1 to 2 hours.

3. Preheat the oven to 300°F. Line two cookie sheets with parchment paper or silicone baking mats. Remove the dough logs from the refrigerator. Slice each log into twelve rounds, about ½-inch thick each.

4. Bake for 30 to 35 minutes, until the edges just begin to brown. Cool the shortbread for 5 minutes in the pan, and then transfer to wire cooling racks to cool completely. Transfer to an airtight lidded container. Consume within 7 to 10 days.

POUND CAKE

A pound cake is so named based on the nearly equal poundages of eggs, butter, sugar, and flour called for in the ingredient list. These four pounds, mixed with a bit of vanilla extract and salt, produce a loaf cake that is without shortcoming on its own. That said, it is just as magnificent saddled up to seasonal or tropical fruits.

For obvious reasons, I love *Steel Magnolias*, a film about a small Southern town and its strong female inhabitants. Whenever I hear Dolly Parton, in her role as Truvy Jones, describe her "Cuppa Cuppa Cuppa" cake as containing a "cup 'o flour, a cup 'o sugar, and a cup 'o fruit cocktail with the juice," I always envision a pound cake, even though that's not the dessert that she is referring to. Having been practically reared on this film and its roster of highly quotable lines, I likely imagined the cake thusly when first viewing the film and, well, first impressions can be hard to shake.

Lucky for all of us, pound cakes contain nary a trace of fruit cocktail. So pay no attention to my inaccurate associations and just start baking this pound cake. From weeknight dinners to baby showers, afternoon luncheons to bridal showers, this will soon be your go-to cake.

SERVING SUGGESTIONS

- *Pound cake possesses a sort of neutral sweet, buttery flavor, so I like to pair it with contrasting yet complementary flavors to keep it from getting too one note. For example, use cubed pound cake in a vanilla pudding and strawberry trifle with fresh basil or mint and loads of freshly whipped cream.*
- *Serve toasted slices with Bourbon Butter Pecan Ice Cream (page 211).*
- *Poach peaches with Riesling and star anise, and serve over warmed slices of pound cake.*

POUND CAKE

· MAKES ONE 9 X 5-INCH POUND CAKE ·

---

4 eggs, yolks and whites separated

1 cup Butter, room temperature, plus extra for greasing (page 194)

1½ cups sugar

2 teaspoons vanilla extract

2 cups all-purpose flour

½ teaspoon sea salt

1. Preheat the oven to 350°F. Liberally butter a 9 x 5-inch loaf pan.
2. Using an electric mixer or whisk, beat the egg whites in a medium bowl until light and billowy.
3. In a separate bowl, using an electric mixer, cream the butter and sugar until light and fluffy, about 3 to 4 minutes. Beat in the vanilla extract.
4. Add the egg yolks, one at a time, beating well and scraping the bowl and beaters with a spatula after each addition. Using a spatula, gently fold in the egg whites until fully incorporated.
5. Whisk together the flour and salt in a medium bowl. Add the flour to the wet mixture, one cup at a time, scraping down the bowl and beaters after each addition.

6. Pour the batter into the prepared pan, using a spatula to spread the batter evenly. Bake for 75 to 80 minutes, until the top is golden brown and a knife inserted into the center comes out clean.

7. Cool in the pan for 15 minutes, then remove from the pan and leave to cool on a rack for 15 minutes longer. Wrap any unused portion in aluminum foil and consume within 5 to 7 days.

POACHED PEARS WITH POUND CAKE, CANDIED BLACK WALNUTS & BOURBON WHIPPED CREAM

· SERVES 8 ·

This dessert is worthy of any dinner party, even the "impress your boss" or "propose to your beloved" kind. It would also be most welcome on the Thanksgiving or holiday dessert table, arranged in a self-serve format. It's essentially what you want to offer when the scent of wood smoke permeates the air and foliage has long since excused itself from branches.

FOR THE PEARS

3 cups pear cider

1 cup water

1 cup packed light brown sugar

Two 3- to 4-inch cinnamon sticks

5 allspice berries

1 whole vanilla bean, split and seeded

4 Bosc or Anjou pears, peeled, cored, and quartered (see Note)

FOR THE WHIPPED CREAM

2 cups heavy cream

2 tablespoons powdered sugar

2 tablespoons bourbon

1 teaspoon vanilla extract

OTHER INGREDIENTS

1 Pound Cake, cut into ½-inch slices

Candied Black Walnuts (page 164)

NOTE: It is essential that your pears still have a bit of firmness to them. Otherwise, if they're overly ripe, they'll turn to mush when poached. A firm fruit with a bit of give when gently pressed is ideal.

1. **PREPARE THE PEARS.** Warm the pear cider, water, and brown sugar in a medium saucepan over medium-high heat. Once the sugar has fully dissolved, but just before the liquid boils, whisk in the cinnamon sticks, allspice berries, and vanilla bean seeds. Add the vanilla bean pod to the poaching liquid.

2. Using a slotted spoon, gently slide the pear pieces into the pan. Cover with a lid, reduce the heat to low, and gently simmer for 15 minutes, carefully flipping them over halfway through the cook time.

3. When the pears are cooked through, remove the lid and with the slotted spoon gently remove the pears from the liquid. Set aside on a large plate or platter.

4. Turn the heat to high, and reduce the liquid volume by half, about 10 to 15 minutes.

5. **PREPARE THE WHIPPED CREAM.** Combine the cream, powdered sugar, bourbon, and vanilla in a large mixing bowl. Using either a mixer or whisk, beat until billowy peaks form. Set aside.

6. **ASSEMBLE THE DESSERT.** Place two slices of pound cake on a dessert plate. Top with two pear pieces and about ¼ cup whipped cream. Scatter a few candied black walnuts over the top. Repeat with the remaining pound cake, pears, and whipped cream. Serve immediately.

BANANA PUDDING TRIFLE WITH CRUSHED PEANUTS & TOASTED COCONUT

· SERVES 6 TO 8 ·

I cannot get enough of trifles. Pound cake, pudding, whipped cream, and fruit. Nothing can go wrong, no matter what type of trifle you intend to serve. Here, bananas, peanuts, and coconut imbue the dish with a sense of Southern hospitality.

FOR THE PUDDING
²/₃ cup sugar

¼ cup cornstarch

4 egg yolks

3¼ cups milk

2 tablespoons Butter (page 194)

2 teaspoons vanilla extract

FOR THE WHIPPED CREAM
2 cups heavy cream

2 tablespoons powdered sugar

1 teaspoon vanilla extract

FOR THE TRIFLE
1 Pound Cake, cut into 1-inch cubes

3 bananas, peeled and cut into about ¼-inch slices

½ cup sweetened coconut, toasted

½ cup roasted and salted peanuts, chopped

1. **PREPARE THE PUDDING.** Combine the sugar and cornstarch in a medium pot. Gradually whisk in the egg yolks and milk until the mixture is smooth.
2. Warm over medium heat and whisk constantly for 5 minutes, until the pudding begins to thicken and bubbles begin forming on the surface.
3. Remove the pan from the heat. Place a fine-mesh sieve over a medium heatproof bowl, and pour the pudding into the sieve, straining off any solids that may have formed.
4. Add the butter and vanilla to the pudding and stir until fully combined. Transfer the bowl to the refrigerator and leave until fully chilled, about 2 to 3 hours.
5. **PREPARE THE WHIPPED CREAM.** Place the cream, powdered sugar, and vanilla in a large mixing bowl. Using either a mixer or whisk, beat until billowy peaks form. Set aside.
6. **ASSEMBLE THE TRIFLE.** Line the bottom of a trifle or 4-quart glass bowl with about one-third of the pound cake cubes. Cover with about one-third of the banana slices, one-third of the pudding, one-third of the whipped cream, one-third of the coconut, and one-third of the peanuts. Repeat to make two more layers, ending with the coconut and peanuts.
7. Transfer to the refrigerator and chill for at least 2 hours before serving. Serve chilled.

LAYER CAKE

————

A no-fail yellow cake should be in the recipe box of any Southern baker (any baker, for that matter). The key to this recipe is having the butter, eggs, and milk all be at room temperature. That way, nothing lumps or coagulates oddly, as might occur with cold ingredients.

Layer cakes have a long history in the South. We have cakes paying tribute to Williamsburg, Virginia, and cakes named for brave Southern women (such as the Lane cake). There are the stack cakes of the impoverished Southern Appalachians, and the mile-high fluffy coconut cakes of the Southern ports of call. I practically taught myself to bake from a young age by ogling my mother's copy of *The Southern Heritage Cakes Cookbook*. Dog-eared pages, a missing spine, and oil drops and frosting splatters throughout offer silent testament to just how frequently I have turned to this book over the course of my life.

Following the base recipe below, I offer recipes for two of my most beloved layer cakes: Salted Caramel Cake and Lime Coconut Cake. To me, these cakes are emblematic of the sweetness of the South. I enjoyed them both as a child living in the region, and, resultantly, deeply associate their flavors with the Southern states. Both require a bit of time, and a good deal of patience. That said, engendering such qualities in oneself only helps in creating a hospitable, warm demeanor, which, after all, is the Southern way.

SERVING SUGGESTIONS

- *This simple butter layer cake is a blank canvas, ready and willing to transform. One idea is to cover the cakes with chocolate buttercream icing, spread raspberry jam between the layers, and top with fresh raspberries.*
- *Cut the cakes into individual pieces and render into petits fours (I first made petits fours when I was eight and remember the occasion with profound clarity!).*
- *Sandwich lemon curd between the layers and frost all over with homemade whipped cream. Scatter candied violets or edible flowers on top.*

LAYER CAKE

· MAKES TWO 9-INCH CAKES ·

---

3 cups all-purpose flour

1 tablespoon baking powder

½ teaspoon sea salt

1 cup whole milk, room temperature

1 tablespoon vanilla extract

1¾ cups sugar

1 cup Butter, room temperature (page 194)

5 eggs, room temperature

1. Preheat the oven to 350°F. Lightly butter and flour two 9-inch round cake pans.
2. Sift together the flour, baking powder, and salt in a medium bowl. Whisk the milk and vanilla in a separate bowl.
3. Cream the sugar and butter in the bowl of an electric mixer until light and fluffy, about 3 to 4 minutes.
4. Add the eggs, one at a time, beating well and scraping the bowl and beaters with a spatula after each addition.
5. On low speed, beat the flour mixture into the butter mixture, alternating with the milk, beginning and ending with the flour. Scrape down the bowl and beaters after each addition.
6. Divide the batter evenly between the prepared pans. Bake for 25 to 30 minutes, until the tops of the cakes are golden brown and a knife inserted into the center comes out clean.
7. Cool in the pans for 10 minutes and then transfer the cakes to wire cooling racks until completely cooled.

LIME COCONUT CAKE

· MAKES ONE 9-INCH LAYER CAKE ·

Growing up, we typically had coconut cake only twice a year, at Christmas and then again at Easter. I have no idea what claims coconut might have on the life of Jesus Christ. All I do know is that coconut cake is too good to only serve twice annually. Here's hoping this cake finds its way into regular rotation in your kitchen.

FOR THE COCONUT

3 cups shredded sweetened coconut

Zest of 1 lime

2 tablespoons fresh lime juice

2 teaspoons lime pulp (see Note)

FOR THE CAKE

Layer Cake, with adjustments per recipe below

Zest of 1 lime

1 teaspoon coconut extract

FOR THE FROSTING

½ cup Butter, room temperature (page 194)

1 cup Cream Cheese, room temperature (page 202)

1 (16-ounce) package powdered sugar, sifted

1 teaspoon vanilla extract

1 teaspoon coconut extract

Pinch of sea salt

NOTE: Lime pulp is obtained by removing the peel and the seeds from the lime, and then coarsely chopping up the remaining membrane and pulpy material.

1. **PREPARE THE COCONUT.** Combine the shredded coconut, lime zest, lime juice, and lime pulp in a medium mixing bowl. Cover with a lid and chill in the refrigerator for 6 to 12 hours.
2. **PREPARE THE CAKES.** Prepare the Layer Cake as per page 233, omitting 1 teaspoon of vanilla (totaling 2 teaspoons instead of 3) and adding the zest of 1 lime and 1 teaspoon coconut.
3. **PREPARE THE FROSTING.** Using an electric mixer, beat together the butter and cream cheese until light and fluffy. Add the powdered sugar, vanilla extract, coconut extract, and salt, and beat until smooth.
4. **ASSEMBLE THE CAKE.** Place one cooled cake layer on a serving plate or cake stand. Spread a bit of frosting on top, and then sprinkle about one-third of the prepared coconut on top.
5. Place the second cake layer on top of the first layer. Spread the remaining frosting across the top and sides of the cake.
6. Sprinkle the remaining coconut across the top of the cake and press it into the sides evenly.
7. Serve immediately or keep in the refrigerator. Rest at room temperature for about 20 minutes before serving.

SALTED CARAMEL CAKE

· MAKES ONE 9-INCH LAYER CAKE ·

I will never forget the first salted caramel cake I tasted. I was at the home of my mother's friend Ayers Henderson in Kinston, North Carolina. Or maybe it was Ayers' mother's house. The house is irrelevant. What matters is the indelible impression that cake made on me. In short, the flavor was incomparable. My pre-teen self didn't know how to describe the taste; all I knew was that I wanted more—immediately. Here's hoping my take produces a similar result in you.

Layer Cake, cooled

3 cups sugar

1 cup Butter (page 194)

1½ cups whole milk, lightly warmed

1 teaspoon vanilla extract

2 teaspoons flake salt (such as Maldon)

1. Place one cake layer on a serving plate or cake stand. Set aside.

2. Place the sugar and butter in a 10-inch cast iron skillet or large heavy-bottomed saucepan. Warm over medium heat, stirring constantly, until the sugar dissolves (this can take 10 to 15 minutes) and begins turning a copper color.

3. Slowly add the warmed milk, stirring constantly. Add the vanilla and continue cooking and stirring for about 15 to 20 minutes, until the mixture reaches the soft ball stage (240°F).

4. Remove the mixture from the heat. With a hand-held mixer (or carefully pour the syrup into the bowl of an electric mixer), beat at medium speed until the mixture becomes thick enough to spread, 3 to 4 minutes.

5. Immediately spread some of the frosting onto the prepared cake layer. Place the second cake layer on top, spread the frosting over the top and sides, and sprinkle the flake salt evenly across the top of the cake.

6. Let the cake set for about 30 minutes before serving. If any of the caramel begins to slide or pool around the bottom of the cake, simply use warm hands to press it back into place.

RESOURCES

Cornmeal

Bob's Red Mill
www.bobsredmill.com

Country Ham

Goodnight Brothers
www.goodnightbrothers.com

Dairy Cultures

Cultures for Health
www.culturesforhealth.com

Grits

Barkley's Mill
www.barkleysmill.com

Anson Mills
www.ansonmills.com

Sorghum

Muddy Pond
www.muddypondsorghum.com

INDEX

ABOUT THE AUTHOR

Ashley English holds degrees in holistic nutrition and sociology. She has worked over the years with a number of nonprofit organizations committed to social and agricultural issues, hosted a bimonthly column for several years in the popular blog Design*Sponge entitled "Small Measures with Ashley," is an ongoing contributor to the quarterly publication *Taproot*, and regularly contributes to a number of regional publications in her area. She is the author of all four books in the Homemade Living Series (*Canning & Preserving*, *Keeping Chickens*, *Keeping Bees*, and *Home Dairy*), as well as *A Year of Pies*, *Quench*, *Handmade Gatherings*, *A Year of Picnics*, and *The Essential Book of Homesteading*.

Ashley has been featured in major publications, including *Food & Wine*, *Country Living*, *Delish*, *Edible Magazines*, and *Anthology*. She has been a repeat guest on Martha Stewart Radio on SiriusFM. Ashley lives in Candler, North Carolina, with her husband, their two sons, and a menagerie of animals, and blogs about her adventures in homesteading, mothering, and beyond at www.smallmeasure.com.

ABOUT THE PHOTOGRAPHER

Johnny Autry became a photographer at age fifteen, when a fifty-year-old press camera with a broken shutter became his constant companion. Since then, Johnny and his wife, Charlotte, have worked with many talented teams to photograph the world of food culture. The mountains of western North Carolina are now his home.